Investing Basics

The Stock Market Guide

for First Time Investors

K.Elizabeth

Committee of the American Bar Association and a Committee of Publishers and Associations.

The information provided herein is stated to be truthful and consistent, in that any liability, in terms of inattention or otherwise, by any usage or abuse of any policies, processes, or

Table of Contents

Bonus Book 1

Bonus Book 2

Introduction

Surviving in the stock market is one of those things in life that require experience, patience, and a particular set of skills in order to excel and succeed. Experience is needed because, well, without it, you'd simply be lost. Patience is needed because the stock market's unpredictable state and constant fluctuations will throw some rather surprising twists and turns your way. Actually, even the most experienced investor will be caught off guard from time to time because of the stock market's volatility, so you'll need to be patient and remain calm throughout all of your financial and economic endeavors. You'll also need a particular set of skills in order to excel and succeed in the financial and economic realm. Fortunately, all of these skills boil down to one thing and one thing only—knowledge.

You'll need to understand what exactly the stock market is, what it does, and what factors cause it to keep stock prices high or cause share prices to decline without any warning whatsoever. You'll need to familiarize yourself with the most common mistakes inexperienced investors make every day in order to prevent yourself from falling into those same traps. Knowledge will help you unlock the *who, what, where, when, why, and how* of the stock market—the questions you need to ask yourself in order to invest in profitable stocks and produce high return rates.

You'll also need to know what your investment options are—are you going to invest in bonds, stocks, penny stocks, mutual funds, or real estate?—and what actions you need to take in order to successfully go about this. You'll also need to do some soul-searching in order to gain a better understanding for *yourself*— what kind of investor are you? Are you willing to take risks in hopes that you reap highly rewarding returns, or are you willing to patiently wait and let your small investments grow over time? What fuels your financial endeavors? What do you want the end result of your investing endeavors to be? How are you going to achieve those endeavors?

Are you starting to feel overwhelmed? Do any of these topics leave you feeling unsure about the stock market and the world of finance and economics? Rest assured—this book will explain, in clear detail, every one of these topics. When you finish reading this book, you'll have a refined sense of clarity about how the stock market works and how to master it. You'll know what common mistakes to avoid when buying, selling, and managing your investments. You'll know what all of your options are, in terms of investment options and who can assist you along the way. You'll even understand just how helpful investing can be when planning ahead for your future, from 5 years down the road to 40.

So spend some time reading and reviewing the following chapters. Take what you learn in the following pages and apply it to your future investing endeavors. You'll soon discover that this short but comprehensive book will boost your confidence about the stock market, will increase your knowledge about the investing world, and will explain simple but highly effective suggestions about how to begin and even manage your time spent in the stock market and the financial world of investing.

Chapter 1: What is an Investment?

We sometimes think that an investment applies only to the stock market. After all, the term "investment" is one of the most popular buzz terms that any individual will hear as soon as they step foot in the financial world.

The term "investment," however, isn't necessarily limited to the stock market. Actually, most, if not all of us, have made some sort of investment at some point in our lives. Have you ever bought a house? That's an investment. Have you ever purchased a car? That's an investment. What about a recent book purchase? That's an investment, too, albeit a small one. Actually, anything you've ever bought can be labeled as an investment, as long as it's doing something productive, helping you out in some way, or allowing you to improve yourself or situations around you. In essence, we're all investors of and in something.

In other words, the term "investment" shouldn't fill you with a sense of dread, confusion, or doubt. It's something you're probably very familiar with, you simply didn't know it. Investments in the financial world work in a similar way. Deciding to invest and taking appropriate actions in doing so can seem like a daunting task, especially without experience and with little to no guidance. Investing certainly doesn't need to be, though.

Investment Defined

In order to relieve any stress or confusions that crop up when thinking about investing or considering the sometimes complex process of doing so, let's begin with a simple definition—one that you can easily wrap your mind around:

- **Investing:** The action or process of investing money with the intention of making a profit.
  - o In some cases, the term "profit" can relate to other things besides money. Investing in books, for example, "profits" your knowledge by educating you on matters otherwise left undiscovered.

- **An investment:** an asset or item that is purchased with the intent that it will generate income or better the future, near or far.

  - In the world of **economics**, an investment would be something that is purchased but is not immediately consumed, as it is intended to produce future wealth or profit.

  - In the world of **finance**, an investment is a monetary asset that is bought in hopes that it will provide an income in the future, and will eventually be sold for a higher price than when it was bought.

What is a Stock Market?

In this book, the type of investments we'll be discussing relate specifically to those that take place in the stock market, a financial arena where stocks can be bought, sold, and exchanged. If you're unfamiliar with the basics of the stock market and the financial environment that exists within the stock market, take a look at the following brief but helpful list that quickly outlines the basics of the stock market. (Hint: familiarizing yourself with the following information will make the rest of this book easier to follow).

- **Stock market:** a market—physical and virtual—in which shares in companies or industries are issued, bought, sold, and traded.

- The stock market allows investors to invest and grow small amounts of money into large ones over a certain period of time. This period of time can be either short or long-term, though certain risks are introduced when investors aim to grow money in short periods of time.

- The stock market provides investors the ability to gain wealth without starting a business or needing to take additional financial risks—it's a more independent and controlled way of building and expanding personal financial wealth.

Chapter 2: The 3 Common Investing Mistakes You Can Easily Avoid

The new or inexperienced investor is bound to make a few mistakes during his or her time in the stock market and world of finance. Mistakes are inevitable, especially in an environment in which stock values are unexpectedly dipping or rapidly increasing. In other words, no investor will make it through their time in the world of finance without encountering at least a couple hurdles and getting bumped and bruised, metaphorically speaking of course, along the way.

Fortunately, there are certain mistakes that *are* entirely avoidable. These are the mistakes that almost all investors make, but can simply avoid if they have the right tools and knowledge *before* they encounter such financial challenges.

You'll find below a short but crucial list of the 3 most common mistakes new or inexperienced investors just like yourself make each and every day in the stock market. Familiarizing yourself with these situations and mistakes, and then recognizing them when you begin to experience them yourself, will help you steer yourself away from falling victim to these all too common, but entirely avoidable, first-time investing mistakes.

Mistake #1: The Wandering Investor

- Investors don't have clear investment goals and outcomes.

Success within the stock market stems from having a pre-established plan that you stick with for the entirety of your time in the financial world. Investors, both inexperienced *and* experienced, all too often fail or struggle to set clear investment goals for themselves *before* they delve into the buying, selling, managing, and exchanging of stocks. When we fail to create investment plans and fail to consider what we want our end result to be, we end up wandering within the financial realm. To avoid this, ask yourself:

- What am I interested in and how can I turn that interest into an investment I care about?

- Where do I plan to be, financially speaking, 6 months from now? 1 year? 5 years? 10 years?

- What are my goals? What do I wish to accomplish with my investment endeavors? What, if any, plans will my profit be put towards?

Mistake #2: The Overly Aggressive Investor

- Investors let the temptation of maximizing short-term returns cloud their judgement.

Entering and participating in the stock market is, of course, about making profit and maximizing profit margins. But there are some loops you need to jump through in order to do so. The backbone of the stock market is to buy low and sell high, yet too many investors reverse this formula—they buy high and sell low in hopes to maximize their short-term returns. When they do this, though, they ignore their less risky long-term investment endeavors. To avoid this, ask yourself:

- Are my investment decisions fueled by greed?

- Are my actions financially risky attempts to increase profit quickly?

- How long do I generally wait before pursuing an investment? Do I observe and analyze the stock for more than a week, or do I immediately invest no matter the price?

Mistake #3: The Easily Swayed Investor

- Investors let what they hear on the news or read in the newspapers influence and even dictate their financial actions and decisions.

The stock market is a constantly fluctuating environment—stocks are always dipping or rising at unprecedented rates. Naturally, news and social media outlets are going to cover these dips and rises. Feel free to watch, but don't let what you hear and read control your financial decisions and actions. Take what you deem valuable and concrete information, and branch off of it. Do your own research on what you hear and read. Consult independent sources, an affiliated brokerage, and analyze charts. Ask yourself:

- What does my research tell me about the stocks I own? What does the news tell me? How is this information similar/different?

- Is this news channel or newspaper a reliable source that is backed by financial experts?

- How recent is the news I hear on TV or read in the newspaper? Has this public information already been factored into the stock market pricings I'm currently see?

Chapter 3: How Much Do You Know About Investing?

Before we go any further, let's stop for a minute. If you're reading this book, you're probably a new or inexperienced investor interested in diving into the world of stocks and investing, right? Maybe you're a more experienced investor seeking to refine his or her current investing skills. Perhaps you're simply curious about the stock market environment and the realm of everything finance and economic.

Regardless of your interests and motivations for reading this book, take some time to complete the following brief but illuminating investing assessment. It'll introduce crucial investing scenarios and situations, and will then ask you, using a True or False style assessment, to provide the best possible answer. The crux of this assessment is this: you'll quickly gain an understanding for where you stand *right now* as an individual interested in stocks and investing. You'll discover where your current strengths lie and where your current weaknesses reside.

Quick Assessment

1. When the stock market experiences a sudden decline, your best course of action is to move all investments to cash and bonds.

    T: _____

    F: _____

2. The CEO of the company you've held stock in for the past 10 years has recently announced his retirement. The new CEO hasn't announced any drastic changes yet, so you should continue to invest and hold stock for that company.

T: _____

F: _____

3. The stock market has been in a rough state for the past couple of months now. To prevent further loss, you should leave your current accounts alone (inactive) until a significant improvement occurs within the marketplace.

T: _____

F: _____

4. Investor A owns shares, bonds, real estate, and has cash in a term deposit. Investor B owns shares in 5 different companies—2 oil development, 1 medical, and 2 technology-based companies. Out of both of these investors, Investor A has a better portfolio.

  T: _____

  F: _____

5. Like the majority of bonds, investing in property is also a virtually risk-free investment opportunity.

  T: _____

  F: _____

6. IPO stands for Initial Public Offering.

  T: _____

  F: _____

7. There are three types of investment opportunities: stocks, bonds, and real estate.

    T: _____

    F: _____

Assessment Follow-up

How confident are you with your answers to the above assessment? The experienced investor should be able to answer most, if not all, of these questions correctly, though the inexperienced investor might not—and that's perfectly okay. That's what this book is here to help you do. In the meantime, however, here's an answer key to the above assessment. Mark your answers. Take note of the questions you got wrong, and be sure to pay close attention to those sections when they appear later on in the book.

1. False. The best thing to do in this situation is to assure your portfolio is well diversified—make sure your eggs aren't in one basket, so to speak.

2. False. Although you might feel comfortable continuing your investment, you should always reassess when new management is introduced.

3. False. Take advantage of the low prices by purchasing several new stocks at low prices.

4. True. A good portfolio is one that has investments across various areas—stocks, bonds, mutual funds, real estate, and cash.

You don't want to limit yourself to just stocks, for example.

5. False. Investing in property carries its risks as well, though the degree of these risks will vary depending on property locations and types.

6. True. An IPO is the first sale of a stock by a private company to a public company. Smaller, newly established companies generally take advantage of this in order to expand and increase capital.

7. False. Though these are three of the most common investment options, mutual funds and cash also count as financial securities and equally excellent investment routes.

Chapter 4: Getting to Know Your Investment Options

One of the major investment-related areas that you'll want to familiarize yourself with *before* you take on any investing endeavors is the different investment options an individual has. You've most likely heard of stocks and perhaps bonds, but are you familiar with the basic function, benefits, and risks of penny stocks, for example? Do you understand the basic premise behind mutual funds? If you're unsure about any or all of these different investment routes, you'll want to spend some time reviewing the following information found in this chapter.

We'll introduce 4 of the most popular investment opportunities currently out there,—stocks, bonds, mutual funds, and penny stocks—will explain the basic characteristics of each one, the advantages associated with each one, and the potential risks that are also intertwined with each of these investment options. Knowing the basic facts about the different investments routes will help you decide which investment opportunity fits your individual needs, personal interests, and unique financial situation.

Stocks

When we think about the stock market, we probably think about stocks, right? The stock market is named after stocks, after all. But what exactly is a stock? Review the following information to find out more.

- **What is it?** The purchase of a **stock** essentially means you own part of a company or corporation, at least from a financial standpoint. You become a shareholder when you invest money into a company.

- **What are the advantages?** When you purchase stock, and therein become a shareholder in a company, you gain certain benefits—you have the ability to vote at shareholder meetings and you are rewarded with certain portions of a company's annual and pre-designated profit.

- **What are the risks?** Stocks can be a fickle investment route, as the stock market is a constantly fluctuating financial environment. Because stocks can drop suddenly—and sometimes never go up again—investors pose the risk of losing large amounts of money in stock investments. However, if a stock does particularly well and sees a rapid increase, the return rate on a stock can be quite profitable and dramatic. Stocks are a risk—sometimes you win, sometimes you lose.

Bonds

Bonds, as you'll soon discover, are a bit different from stocks. These differences between stocks and bonds come in several different areas.

- **What is it?** Bonds revolve around a company's debt to a shareholder (an investor). Essentially, an investor lends money to a company for a pre-established period of time, and in return, the company pays interest on the money you've lent it.

- **What are the advantages?** Bonds are excellent investment opportunities because they carry little to no risks, making bonds unlike any other investment option currently out there.

- **What are the risks?** Bonds don't necessarily have risks; they have disadvantages. Because it's a very safe investment opportunity, return rates on bonds typically aren't very high. In other words, you're not going to "make bank" off a bond, especially with short-term bonds. Profit in bond investments come slowly and after an extended period of time, usually upwards of 10 or more years if you're seeking to make a significant monetary return.

Mutual Fund

Inexperienced investors sometimes forget about the existence of mutual funds for some odd reason. However, mutual funds are also great investment routes, especially for individuals who are short on time.

- **What is it?** A mutual fund is when a group of investors pool their cash assets together to pay a financial expert to research, select, and manage investments for the group.

- **What are the advantages?** Mutual funds are advantageous to investors who aren't able to commit a reasonable amount of their time to researching and pursuing investments in stocks and bonds. Hiring a financial professional also reduces the amount of work on your end, as well as reduces the amount of times you find yourself in financially challenging or crippling situations in the stock market. In essence, there should be less investing mistakes made since you have a professional handling your group's investment endeavors.

- **What are the risks?** The risks with mutual funds depend upon the investment route your group and financial expert decide upon. If your mutual fund revolves primarily around stocks, for example, you increase your financial risks. If it focuses on bonds, on the other hand, you significantly reduce your risk, if not eliminate it.

Penny Stock

Again, this is another investment opportunity that often goes overlooked. It's not as common as the previous three, especially among those looking to invest larger amounts of money, though it still proves to be worth your time in exploring and learning more about.

- **What is it?** Like its name suggests, penny stocks are common stocks that are valued at less than a dollar. Actually, most penny stocks are valued somewhere around $0.10 per share.

- **What are the advantages?** Because penny stocks are *so* inexpensive, investors are able to invest in many different stocks without needing to sacrifice large amounts of money. Doing so is beneficial because it allows them to diversify their portfolio (spread their investments out among different areas so that if one stock fails, all your money isn't lost).

- **What are the risks?** Penny stocks are quite unpredictable and can be quite volatile, meaning they change constantly and can fluctuate quite drastically without any warning. A penny stock investor needs to be able to think quickly on his or her feet, and needs to feel comfortable taking financial risks.

Chapter 5: Getting Started—Opening Your Brokerage Account

The new or inexperienced investor is highly encouraged to seek the help of a financial professional or economic expert when starting their journey into the stock market and financial realm. Brokers and brokerage firms are the individuals and licensed organizations that will help your transition into the financial marketplace go a lot smoother. Really, look into this option.

Think of a broker as a financial tutor. They're there to teach you new skills, guide you through challenging times, give advice on ways to improve, double check your decisions and actions, and provide additional tools, resources, and services that will help you grow into an experienced, knowledgeable, and successful investor.

What is a Broker and What Do They Do?

But what *exactly* does a broker do, you ask? Well, first and foremost, a broker is:

- A licensed financial professional who either handles the buying and selling of stocks/investments when you ask them to, or who helps and closely guides you throughout the entirety of your investment endeavors.

There are, however, two different forms of brokers: **full-service brokers** and **discount brokers**. The full-service broker is generally assigned to individuals looking to invest large sums of money into various securities, usually an amount of $50,000 or more. Because the investment sum is rather large, full-service brokers provide a wide range of services and resources, and are there to guide you and consult with you along the way. Discount brokers, on the other hand, are typically assigned to individuals who seek to invest small amounts of money, usually a minimum of $500-$1,000. They generally do not provide additional services and free consultations like full-service brokers do. They are simply there to handle the buying and selling process when you ask them to. Essentially, you tell, they do.

Before and During Opening a Brokerage Account

Whether you want to admit it or not, you'll probably need a little hand-holding when you first enter the stock market. Opening and using your brokerage account will solve this issue quite nicely. Once you've done your research and have found a brokerage firm that you trust and feel comfortable with, you'll need to:

- **Have at least 6 months' salary in your savings.** This is always a good rule of thumb. It's a good idea to have money in your savings to begin with, and having money in your savings will reduce the financial burden that comes with filling out an application and paying an application fee (continue reading to learn more about this process).

- **Do your research.** Find out what services different brokers offer. Pay close attention to the fine print on websites. Look for information regarding:
    - o If a broker charges maintenance fees
    - o If a broker charges monthly fees
    - o If phone calls are charged
    - o What a broker's commission rate is

- What you'll be charged for with each exchange

- If a broker offers free checking perks or bill-pay services

- **Meet potential brokers and conduct mini-interviews.** You want your interests, goals, and desired outcomes to align with your broker, so be sure to ask them the questions found above. Ask for contact information for current or previous clients. Remember, your broker will be managing your finances and therefore your future financial stability, so be sure to find one who is communicative, reliable, and trustworthy.

- **Fill out an application and pay an application fee.** This fee is usually $1,000, and can sometimes be an investment in and of itself. You'll find it hard to find a brokerage that doesn't charge an application fee for filling out an application, though some online firms have significantly lower application fees, if not free. You'll need to decide what kind of interaction you're looking for—if you want a *human* to communicate with on a daily basis, stick to a broker. If you're okay with more independence and don't need to consult with someone, an online brokerage account might be for you. Whatever you do, don't let the thought of putting down a $1,000 application deposit deter you from seeking the financial help you're in need of.

Contact and stay in frequent contact with your assigned broker. Again, the type of broker you're assigned—full-service or discount—will depend upon your investing plans and goals. Once you've been assigned a broker, he or she will help you take it from there.

Chapter 6: I Opened an Account, Now What?

If you've been assigned a full-service broker after creating your brokerage account, this chapter might not be entirely useful. Your broker will be able to advise you on your financial situations in more detail than what the space of this chapter allows. If you've been assigned a discount broker, however, this chapter is *very* important to you.

A discount broker won't generally offer consultation services or advice during your investing endeavors, so the new or inexperienced investor will be left out in the dark to fend for himself or herself in many cases. Don't let this happen to you. You'll need to know when the best time to buy a stock is, when the best time to sell a stock is, and everything in between. Familiarizing yourself with the most important dos and don'ts of buying and selling stocks will help you achieve success in the stock market. That's what we'll discuss in this chapter.

The Dos and Don'ts of Buying Stock

Making decisions regarding when to buy stock can be quite complicated and stressful, though it doesn't necessarily need to be. You'll want to always approach buying situations with caution, of course, but you shouldn't let your worries deter you from pursuing purchase opportunities. The following 3 sets of buying dos and don'ts will help shave away some of your buying hesitancies, clarify any misconceptions, and help you become a more confident investor when it comes to buying stock.

Do: Buy stocks from companies with gradual and positive growth over extended periods of time.

Don't: Buy stocks from companies that have grown exponentially over short period of time, or don't allow public access to financial history reports or annual financial reports.

Do: Research and invest in companies that have unique business models and corporate advantages over competitors.

Don't: Invest in a company simply because *you* like their product. Remember: a large amount of investors and consumers need to like the company's product, too, in order to maintain share purchase rates and keep the value of the stock high, or at least maintain it. Perhaps more importantly, consumers and investors need to *keep* liking the product a company offers in order for the company to continue their positive growth in profit and revenue.

Do: Diversify your investments. Spread your investment interests out among several different areas. A somewhat aggressive investor is who willing to take financial risks in order to gain potentially high return profits might want to invest 70% of his cash assets into 2 or 3 different stocks, and 30% of his cash assets into bonds. A more conservative investor, on the other hand, might want to invest 50% of her cash assets into bonds, 40% into stocks, and leave 10% of cash assets in the bank.

Don't: "Time" the market. Waiting for the absolute best time to act and invest is pointless—there isn't really a *best* time to buy in the stock market.

The Dos and Don'ts of Selling Stock

Much like with buying stock, selling stock has a particular set of dos and don'ts as well. Again, your discount broker might not have the time or resources to help you out or consult with you during this process, so be sure to review the following information.

Do: Sell your investments if you experience a negative profit for more than 2 financial quarters.

Don't: Hang on to investments with the *hope* that they will get better and prices will rise again. If a stock is gradually falling for an extended period of time, let it go. Take the profit you've gained over time and invest elsewhere.

Do: Pay attention to fees that come along with selling and trading stocks—they'll add up. Refer back to Chapter 5's discussion regarding what to look for in the fine print of websites when shopping for a broker.

Don't: Let your personal situations or emotions affect your financial decisions. No matter the situation, it's vital that you stick to the financial plan you hopefully created and set before you pursued any investment opportunities.

Conclusion

If you're able to get your hands on a full-service stock broker, do so by all means. They'll be extraordinarily helpful during your initial immersion into the stock market and financial arena. Most new or inexperienced investors won't have access to the services, tools, resources, and consultation opportunities that full-service brokers offer, however, as their investment sums will generally be less than $50,000, and understandably so. If you find yourself in a situation such as this—confused about the workings of the stock market but left without helpful resources—then this book has hopefully helped out get started.

This book by no means offers a comprehensive look into the techniques and tools needed in order to survive in the stock market. What it does offer, however, is basic information that new or inexperienced investors need to get started. And although this book is relatively short, you should have learned a reasonable amount in such little time.

That is, in Chapter 1, we explored the basics of investing and the stock marketing, providing a few helpful definitions for each term. With this knowledge in mind, Chapter 2 introduced the 3 most common mistakes inexperienced investors make, therein giving you the warning and knowledge necessary to avoiding these unproductive and harmful situations in the first place. Chapter 3 then helped you gain an understanding for where you currently stood in terms of investing and stock market knowledge. The short assessment should have highlighted the areas you excel at and the financial topics in which you needed to improve. Following that, Chapter 4 then delved into the different investment opportunities you as an investor have— investing in stocks, bonds, mutual funds, and penny stocks. Chapter 5 might be the most important chapter, since its discussion about brokers is what will either make or break your time in the stock market and financial arena. In other words, you're highly encouraged to find a broker during your journey into the investing world. Chapter 6 then provided some simple but extremely effective dos and don'ts suggestions about buying and selling stocks.

At this point, we've covered a lot of the basic information relating to buying and selling stocks, managing your investment endeavors, and successfully surviving in the stock market. Now is the time that you should put your newly discovered knowledge and skills to the test. Apply what you've learned in this book as you begin your investing journey. Consult the suggestions throughout this book when making investment decisions and taking financial actions.

I wish you the best of luck with your investing endeavors, whatever those may be, and wherever they may take you.

Retirement Planning

6 Simple Actions You Can Take Right Now That Will Help You Retire With Enough Money

K. ELIZABETH

and a Committee of Publishers and
Associations.

In no way is it legal to reproduce, duplicate, or
transmit any part of this document in either
electronic means or in printed format.
Recording of this publication is strictly
prohibited and any storage of this document is
not allowed unless with written permission
from the publisher. All rights reserved.

The information provided herein is stated to
be truthful and consistent, in that any liability,
in terms of inattention or otherwise, by any
usage or abuse of any policies, processes, or
directions contained within is the solitary and

The trademarks that are used are without any consent, and the publication of the trademark is without permission or backing by the trademark owner. All trademarks and brands within this book are for clarifying purposes only and are the owned by the owners themselves, not affiliated with this document. Money-back Guarantee: If you are not satisfied with the book for any reason, you may also get a refund within 7 days of purchase. Click *Your Account* and select *Action* directly next to the book you'd like to receive a refund for, and click on *Return for refund.*

Table of Contents

Introduction

Retirement. For some, it's the word that gets us through the monotonous years of our lackluster careers. For others, it's the word that encourages us to envision glimpses of our mysterious future. Regardless of the excitement or dread the word inspires in us, however, retirees are all in the same boat— we've got to figure out a new life after our working life has ended. *Will I finally fulfill my life long goal of traveling Europe after retirement? Will I finally be able to help my daughter and son-in-law out by babysitting the grandkids before and after school?* Before we retire, however, we all need to complete one underrated yet extremely crucial step: math. Although our newly discovered, non-working lives give us plenty of free time and opportunities to pick up new hobbies, we need to determine if we can even *afford* the retired life we wish to live. After all, we can't simply stop working and expect to watch the retirement money pile into our bank accounts, at least not without taking the right pre-retirement actions. And with today's economy, these pre-retirement steps become especially crucial.

It might surprise you,—and not in a good way—that the average 50 year old retiree has an estimated $42,000 in savings. Sure, $42,000 peacefully sitting in your bank sounds great on the surface, but it's certainly not enough when we consider that the average length of retirement is 18 years. *18 years.* Without taking into account *some* of the money you'll receive from Social Security benefits and pensions, you're expected to live off of $42,000 for *18 years.* Even the most optimistic retiree will see the absurdity in this, which is why doing the math *before* you retire is vital. You need to make sure that your pre-retirement actions guarantee you retire with enough money—enough money that'll last you an average of 18 years.

That's what this book is all about—taking the right pre-retirement actions that ensures you're able to retire with enough money. What constitutes "enough money" will, of course, depend on you. But no matter your interpretation, you'll find some excellent resources throughout this book that'll help you achieve it.

One of the most common reasons why people struggle or fail to retire with enough savings is that they simply don't know their options— even the most basic options. Many don't know the rule of thumb that suggests a retiree should retire with 8x his or her annual income in their bank account *before* retirement. We'll discuss this. Many don't know that Social Security and pensions aren't the reliable sources of income that they once were or are made out to be. We'll quickly discuss this. Many don't know how 401(k) work and therefore don't receive their full benefits. We'll explore the benefits of this. Many don't understand how crucial it is to entire retirement mortgage and debt-free. We'll discuss this as well.

Retirement is filled with uncertainties,—what you'll do with your free time, what hobbies you'll pick up, what long deserved vacations you'll treat yourself to, what luxurious indulgences you'll treat yourself to—but how you financially support yourself shouldn't be.

Chapter 1: Know the Statistics

Thousands of hardworking, ambitious, and dedicated retirees in America *alone* struggle with finances after they've retired, not because they're financially irresponsible, but because they simply didn't know all their options *before* retirement. These misunderstandings happen more than you'd think, unfortunately. Information surrounding retirement plans and programs is oftentimes convoluted. The promise of Social Security and pension benefits are often exaggerated.

To avoid entanglement in the disorientating web of retirement information, you should take some time to learn the facts—the facts about the average length of retirement, how much the average retiree truly needs to have saved, and how many people struggle to survive on Social Security and pension benefits alone. You'll find an overwhelming amount of information by doing a quick internet search, but I've narrowed down some crucial statistics here that I think every retiree or potential retiree needs to know and fully understand about retirement. If you haven't yet retired, this chapter will be especially important to you—by familiarizing yourself with this information, you're taking the first step in *not* becoming one of the statistics (usually a good sign in the universe of retirement).

The Bad Stats

Again, there's an overwhelming amount of statistics out there regarding retirement, but I've selected a handful that prove to be the most informative:

- The average retirement age is 63.

- The average savings of a 64 year old—working or retired—is $45,500.

- A retired individual will spend over $100,000 on medical expenses over the course of 20 years.

- 35% of Americans don't have any retirement savings.

- 4% of retirees have enough money saved to maintain their pre-retirement lifestyles.

- When asked about retirement, 60% of individuals believed they may have to delay their retirement because of the current economic recession.

- More than 60% of retirees are financially dependent on Social Security, family and friends, and charities.

- 75% of prescription drug purchases come from retirees over the age of 50.

The Good Stats

Fortunately, retirement doesn't *always* mean you'll face financial challenges or hardship if you haven't properly saved an adequate amount of money before retirement. Unfortunately, the "good" statistics that reflect financial activities among retirees are significantly less. Nonetheless, take a look at the following statistics. Let the thought of becoming part of *these statistics* motivate you into taking the appropriate actions that lead to your retirement success.

- More than 45% of all auto sales are to retired individuals.

- 80%—yes, 80%—of all luxury and tropical travel purchases come from retirees over the age of 50.

- At least half of all American families now have retirement accounts.

- The confidence in retirement resources between generation X (born between 1965-1980) and the Millennial generation (1981-1993) has increased from 53% to 72%.

What the Statistics Suggest

So, what does all this mean? *What does it mean that only 4% of retirees have enough money saved to maintain their pre-retirement lifestyle, but that more than 50% of all families have retirement accounts?* If you find yourself asking questions similar to this, here's a helpful breakdown of what these statistics mean:

Stat: 50% of all families have retirement accounts but only 4% of retirees have enough money saved to maintain their pre-retirement lifestyle.

- **Explanation:** This shows that more and more families are becoming aware of the importance of pre-retirement planning and saving, but that they're probably not taking full advantage of the benefits IRAs and 401(k)s offer.

Stat: 80% of all luxury and tropical travel purchases come from retirees over the age of 50, but more than 60% of all retirees are dependent on Social Security benefits, friends and family, and charitable donations.

- **Explanation:** There seems to be a gap here. How can all this retiree money go toward vacations if 60% of retirees are looking to others for financial help? Here's the thing: only a select number of retirees make up that 80%, ones will thousands upon thousands saved in their accounts. This 80% comes from the 1% (only 1% of retirees are considered wealthy).

Chapter 2: The 8x Rule

Retirement Fact #1*: Less than half of all Americans take the time to calculate how much they'll need to save for retirement.*

What it means*: Thousands upon thousands of Americans enter retirement financially blind.*

_____

_____

You can know *all* about retirement,—what to expect, what not to expect, what you're going to do when you retire—but you won't be able to retire with enough in your savings on this knowledge alone. In other words, retiring with enough money is all about doing your calculations. Perhaps more importantly, these calculations need to happen *before* you retire, not *after*. The problem is, however, that individuals don't often know what these calculations should entail. *Should I calculate my current monthly income and compare that to my income after retirement in order to better understand my financial situation? Do I also need to factor in my monthly expenses?* The truth is that there's a great deal you'll need to factor in. You'll slowly discover these elements throughout the book as you continue to read, but there's an incredibly helpful piece of advice that many economists and financial experts suggest to potential retirees. And it's quite a simple calculation, too.

The Financial Expert's Golden Rule to Retirement Savings

If you're thinking about retiring and haven't yet met with a financial expert who specializes in retirement planning, do so as soon as you can. This is a financial *must*. Retirement proves to be such a challenging action because we just don't know a lot of the basic components of retirement. A financial expert will help demystify retirement and correct any misconceptions you have about pre-retirement, the retire process, and your life after you've retired.

In the meantime, financial experts have a great suggestion for anyone looking to save "enough money" before they retire. Their advice?

- You should have at least **8 times your current annual income** saved in your bank *before you even <u>think</u> about retirement.*

Breaking Down the 8x Rule

To many people, this sounds like an impossible feat. The thought of paying bills, living expenses, and other monthly costs can make it seem nearly impossible to save up such a large amount of money, but it's important that you strive to meet this goal to the best of your ability. Here's a breakdown of why having 8 times your annual income saved *before* retirement is crucial.

Let's estimate that your yearly pre-retirement income is $50,000. Let's not consider retirement benefits (Social Security, pension, 401(k)s) at the moment, and let's only factor in minimal expenses.

Current Savings	Yearly Expenses	New Savings Amount After Expenses
1. $50,000 (start)	Mortgage: $15,000	$35,000
2. $35,000	Utilities: $8,000	$27,000

3. $27,000	Food: $6,000	$21,000
4. $21,000	Car: $1,500	$19, 500
5. 19,500	Other: $10,000	$9,500
6. $9, 500 (end)		

Do you see just how quickly your money, even $50,000 a year, seems to run out? This is why it's important to have *at least* 8 times your annual income—in this case, $400,000—saved up before retirement.

But remember: we simply added in the basic expenses. Your mortgage might be higher, your utilities *are* probably higher, you might spend more money per year on food if you enjoy cooking or entertaining guests often, you might spend more money on gas per year if it takes more than $30 to fill your tank every 2 weeks, if you get takeout more than once a week, if you decide to complete home renovations, buy new furniture, or have medical costs not covered by insurance.

- At this rate, having 8 times your annual income saved in your bank account means you can live a **minimal lifestyle** for just over **11 years**. But what happens after that? Sure, Social Security benefits will help defray *some* costs, but not as much as you'd probably think.

With all that being said, there suddenly doesn't seem to be as much wiggle room as you thought, even having saved an impressive

$400,000 (8 times your annual income).

Chapter 3: Learn to Love Your 401(k)

Retirement Fact #2: The money you receive annually from Social Security benefits will amount to, on average, 40% of your annual income before retirement.

What it means: You can't be financially dependent on your Social Security benefits after retirement. In order to retire with enough money, you'll need to take another approach. The 401(k) proves to be a valuable option.

When we talk about retirement, there are a few common buzz words that generally crop up during conversations: Social security, pensions, 401(k)s and IRAs are among the most common. A highly knowledgeable retiree will be familiar with each of these benefit and savings programs and how they work. Unfortunately, there are many misconceptions about each of these programs that are currently in circulation, which means more and more retirees are receiving information that just simply isn't true. One of the first steps *before* you retire will involve you becoming familiar with each of these programs—Social Security, pension, 401(k)s, and IRAs—and learning how you can benefit most from each.

But because we're talking about how to retire with enough money, we'll focus on one crucial saving program for now— the 401(k). We won't focus much on Social Security because, well, it's simply no longer a reliable financial source that retirees can depend on. In fact, studies show that annual Social Security benefits equal, on average, only 40% of an individual's annual income before retirement. In other words, depending on Social Security benefits *won't* help you retire with enough money. So then, what *will* help you retire with enough money? Well, the 401(k) proves to be a highly reliable source, so let's spend some time learning about it.

The Benefits of the 401(k)

Every working individual should be familiar with the 401k—how it works, how you benefit from it, and what you need to do in order to get the most out of it. If you're already familiar with it, that's great. You may want to quickly review the following information, then move on to Chapter 4, 5, and 6. If you're not too familiar with the 401(k), or simply want to demystify any questions you have about it, then this section is here to help. Here's some of the (basic) information you *need* to know about your 401(k) before you move forward with your retirement planning.

- **What is it?** A 401(k) is a common retirement savings program that is sponsored by your employer. Employees—you—are allowed to save and invest certain percentages of their paycheck into their 401(k) without tax deductions—taxes will instead be paid when you withdraw money from your account.

- **How does it work?** In order to get the best results, you'll want to dedicate as much of your paycheck as allowed toward your 401(k) savings. Almost every 401(k) offers a "matching funds program," which means when you put a certain amount—generally 3% of your paycheck—into your account, your employer will match that contribution, essentially doubling the amount.

- **What are the restrictions?** Unfortunately, you might have to wait a while before you can gain access to the money your employer contributes to the account. You'll need to be employed by your employer for a certain amount of time before gaining access. Your own monetary contributions will, of course, be available, though there are many intricate rules regarding when you can withdraw your money, especially *before* retirement—this is often also followed by penalties. There's also another drawback: you're only allowed to contribute a certain amount of money annually, per the IRS. This annual limit is $18,000 (as of 2015) before you turn 50. After 50, you're allowed to contribute another "catch-up" amount of $6,000 per year, allowing you to increase your annual contribution to $24,000.

So, what does all this mean?

Essentially, a 401(k) won't allow you to save unlimited amounts of money in your account before you retire, but it *does* help you save. What you contribute annually will determine whether you're able to save a small or significant amount of money, but no matter the amount, your 401(k) will provide *some* financial security, all without noticing a significant difference in your paycheck. What's also great about the 401(k) is that if you stay with your current employer long enough, they'll match your contributions. When done correctly, you'll double your contributions without needing to lift a finger.

Simple 401(k) Breakdown

Here's why it's great:

- Let's say your annual income is $50,000 and your employer matches 50% of your contributions.

- Let's also say that your monthly 401(k) contribution will be 3% ($1,500) of your paycheck.

  With each passing year, your 3% monthly contributions will amount to $18,000 (the annual limit).

Your annual contribution	Employer's "Match"	Total Savings

Year 1:	$9,000	$27,000
$18,000		
Year 2:	$9,000	$54,000
$18,000		
Year 3:	$9,000	**$81,000**
$18,000		

This is of course a simplified breakdown, but it still does quite an effective job of showing just how much your 401(k) saving account will benefit you and help you retire with a sufficient and even comfortable amount of money. Understanding the benefits (and restrictions) of your 401(k) is crucial, but it's also crucial that you eagerly embrace your 401(k) and make it an active member of your pre-retirement life. It's one of the most effective and guaranteed ways to retire with enough money.

For more information on choosing a 401(k), establishing a 401(k), and contributing, maintaining, and terminating a 401(k), try:

- https://www.irs.gov/Retirement-Plans/401k-Plans

Chapter 4: What's Your Retirement Lifestyle?

Retirement Fact #3: A recent study to determine the best and worst states for retirement, which took into account living costs, healthcare, taxes, and weather (among other factors), found that South Dakota, Colorado, and Utah were among the top states to retire to. Florida, the stereotypical retirement spot, didn't even place among the top 25.

No matter what you plan to do during retirement—surround yourself with children and grandchildren, fulfill your lifelong desire to travel the world and spend weeks with your feet dug deep into the warm sand of tropical beaches, or anything in between—you'll need to make sure you have enough money to do it. In other words, retirees looking to live a quiet and quaint life won't need to have saved the same amount as retirees looking to explore the world and treat themselves to life's well-deserved luxuries.

As you prepare to start your *pre-retirement* savings calculations,—such as the 8x rule we discussed earlier in Chapter 2—you'll need to spend some time reflecting on the life you want to live after retirement. Do you prefer the humble atmosphere of being surrounded by family and friends, or do you prefer a retired life full of adventure and luxury? Either is, of course, perfectly acceptable—you've been working for 30+ years, so you deserve the opportunity to do what *you* now want to do. However, you'll need to keep a few crucial questions in mind as you reflect upon your visions of retired life:

Important Questions You Need to Ask Yourself

1. Will the amount that I have saved when I retire support my retirement endeavors?

- In order to answer this question, you'll need to have **at least a general idea** of what you'd like to do after you've retired. As you're hopefully starting to see, retiring with enough money isn't *just* about performing monetary calculations; it's also about embracing the self-reflection process. You need to have an understanding **for what you value most** and how that'll play a role in your retirement. If you value traveling, for example, you'll need to think about where'd like to visit and for how long. Put together some rough calculations of your travel costs, add them to your yearly retirement expenses, and see if your savings will support your endeavors *before* you travel.

2. If the amount I've saved *doesn't* support the retired life I want to create for myself, how will I either 1.) Find financial support that *will* let me pursue these endeavors, or 2.) Adjust my future plans so that my savings *do* support my retirement endeavors?

- If you come across this common problem, don't worry yourself too much. There are a few viable financial options you may want to consider, such as your 401(k) savings. If you actively took advantage of your 401(k), you should have quite a bit of savings in your account. If you do plan on traveling and/or indulging in frequent, well-deserved luxuries, you may want to consider using your 401(k) to support your basic essentials, and then your personal retirement savings to fund the more luxurious elements of your retired life. Whatever you chose, it's vital that you secure dependable financial support for your basic living expenses *before* you indulge in the more luxurious elements of retirement.

3. Have I also taken into account the necessary living expenses that will remain with me even during retirement, such as current debts (mortgage, credit cards), my monthly expenses (utilities, food, entertainment, transportation costs)?

- Before you do anything, really,—travel abroad, buy a new car, renovate your home—you need to be sure that you can support your *basic* needs *first*. If all expenses are paid for, then your remaining money is yours to do with as you wish. Just remember to be financially responsible—your savings will need to last quite a few years.

The 4% Rule

For those still struggling to determine how their retirement lifestyle choice will match up with their savings, embracing the 4% rule might be a great idea. Essentially, the 4% rule works like this:

- You can withdraw 4% a year from your savings account for the next 25 years without outliving your money. Here's how it breaks down:

- Let's say you saved **$500,000** (this money can come from your own personal savings and/or your 401(k). We won't factor in Social Security benefits or pension incomes, which will give you a bit more wiggle room).
- 4% of $500,000 is **$20,000.** This means you'll have $20,000 to live off of each year for the next 25 years. (The average retirement length is 18 years).

- So, you'll want to consider:
  - Will **$20,000** a year cover my debts (mortgage and/or credit card payments for 12 months),

yearly living expenses (food, transportation, utilities, entertainment, etc), *and* the retirement activities I want to do?

- Or, for those who were able to retire with a more generous amount in their savings account, your financial situation might look more like this:
  - Say instead that you saved **$1,000,000.**
  - With the 4% rule, this means you can withdraw **$40,000** each year for the next 25 years without outliving your savings.
  - Again, you'll want to consider if this amount adequately covers

your debts, yearly living expenses, and the retirement activities you wish to do.

Chapter 5: Paying off Your Mortgage before

Retirement Fact #4: Financial experts estimate that the average person will need at least 90% of their pre-retirement income to maintain their standard way of living and make mortgage payments after they have stopped working.

No matter our age, a mortgage can be one of the biggest debts that loom over our hardworking heads for years—*years*—at a time. When we make minimal payments each month on lengthy 20-30 year mortgages, decades of our lives are spent dishing out our money into intangible bank accounts. As many would suspect, this process becomes even worse when we no longer have the income we once had. Although we do still have an income source when we retire—generally from Social Security benefits and pensions, for some—it's not nearly as much as it was when we were working.

As we learned earlier, the average retiree's annual income is only 40% of what he or she earned while working. What this means for anyone who is still paying off a mortgage or major debt during retirement is this: After retirement, you'll need to make monthly mortgage payments with only 40% of your pre-retirement income, which probably means you'll need to pull money from your personal savings or 401(k) savings in order to do so. For most, even the mere thought of doing this sounds dreadful. You've worked for 30+ years and have actively contributed to a savings account that you hoped would support your *enjoyable* retirement endeavors—you *don't* want to see portions of your hard-earned savings go toward paying off debts.

To avoid the unnecessary draining of your personal savings to mortgage payments or debt pay-offs, you'll want to do *all you can do* to pay off your debt *before* retirement. Yes, it can absolutely be a hard process, but it certainly is a feasible task for the committed and motivated individual. Think about it this way:

- ❖ **Yes,** you *can* retire with enough money without paying off your mortgage or other debts before retirement, **but** making these payments during retirement will drain your savings and can make it so you *no longer* have enough money during retirement.

- ❖ **Yes**, Paying off a mortgage or debt *before* retirement *can* make it harder to contribute to your pre-retirement savings account, **but** doing so will also drastically cut your monthly/annual expenses after you retire. You won't experience the sight of a quickly draining savings account, and the money you *do* have saved can be put towards things you actually *enjoy*.

The Benefits of Pre-Retirement Debt Pay-offs

Still not convinced that paying off your mortgage or other debts *before* retirement is an effective way of retiring with enough money? Well, here's a simple breakdown that'll hopefully help you see the benefits of doing so. (To make this example a bit less complicated, I didn't factor in annual Social Security benefits or possible pensions. I just want to show, in simplest terms, how you'll benefit.

Scenario #1: Retiring with a Mortgage:

Let's say you retire at age 55 with $500,000 in savings. You buy a new, downsized home for $300,000. Your mortgage is for 25 years, which means your minimum **monthly** mortgage payments will be **$1,000.** Here's what your breakdown looks like:

- You're retiring young, so you take advantage of the 4% rule (Chapter 4) to ensure your savings don't run out. 4% of $500,000 is $20,000. You have **$20,000** to live off each year.

Savings Account Total:	$500,000
Year 1: "Income" using 4% rule:	$20,000

- Your minimum monthly mortgage payment is $1,000, which means you must pay at least $12,000 to your mortgage each year.

Year	Mortgage Payment	
Year 1: $20,000	Year 1: $12,000	**$ After Mortgage $8,000**

- At this point, almost half—*half*—of your annual "income" has gone toward paying off your mortgage. Yet, there are quite a few other annual expenses you'll need to pay as well (food, utilities, other bills, transportation, other expenses).

Year	Annual Expenses	
Year 1: $8,000	Utilities: $4,000	
	Food: $4,000	
	Car: $1,000	
	Other: $5,000	After basic expenses: -$6,000

Yikes, looks like you'll need to pull an **additional $6,000** from your savings account in order to cover *just* your monthly expenses.

Scenario #2: Retiring without a Mortgage

Using the same background information as the previous scenario, let's see how your annual expenses break down when you've paid off your mortgage *before* retirement:

- Again, you're retiring young, so you'll want to take advantage of the 4% rule. 4% of $500,000 is $20,000. You have **$20,000** to live off each year.

Savings Account Total:	$500,000	
Year 1: "Income" using 4% rule:	$20,000	

- You don't have a mortgage to worry about, so let's factor in your annual basic expenses:

Year	Annual Expenses	
Year 1: $20,000	Utilities: $4,000	
	Food: $4,000	
	Car: $1,000	
	Other: $5,000	After basic expenses: +$6,000

- Even after paying off your basic annual expenses, you have an additional $6,000 (compared to the -$6,000 with mortgage payments) in your savings that you can put toward whatever you so desire.

So, How Do I Do it?

Paying off a mortgage or debt is a process in and of itself, so we unfortunately won't be discussing the (surprisingly simple) details of successfully completing these payoffs. However, I'd highly recommend that you look further into this topic, especially if you fear that your mortgage payments or debt will haunt you throughout your retirement. I'd recommend browsing through one of my other books, *How We Became Mortgage-Free: 12 Proven and Effective Tips that will Help You Become Mortgage-Free Without Sacrificing Your Lifestyle.* It details my own family's experience with paying off our $373, 300 mortgage in just over 4 years, and includes everything you need to know in order to find success with eliminating your debts before retirement.

Chapter 6: The Simple Dos and Don'ts of Retirement

So far, we've covered a few simple yet highly effective ways that'll help you retire with enough money in your savings account. Embracing the 8x rule, taking advantage of all the benefits your 401(k) has to offer, approaching your annual expenses using the 4% rule, and paying off your mortgage *before* you retire have all proven to be valuable concepts for future retirees. I've hopefully sparked a few ideas for you throughout this brief book, and I hope to leave you with just a few more.

The Dos of Retirement

When we discuss retirement options with others, we're often bombarded with a list of retirement and pre-retirement dos and don'ts. Unless you've got a pen and paper readily available, you're bound to miss some helpful suggestions during conversations. To help with this, I've included a brief list of some valuable *dos* of retirement that you should adopt.

- **Do: Ask your employer about pension opportunities**. Although 96% of Americans receive Social Security benefits after retirement, only a small percentage receive pensions. However, you should never assume that you don't have a pension opportunity. Just ask. They're not generally dependable financial resources, but they can provide *some* extra income.

- **Do: Look into IRAs.** An "Individual Retirement Account," which comes in three different forms—Traditional, Roth, and Rollover—allows individuals to save for retirement without taxation or with tax deferral. They're similar to 401(k)s and provide great pre-retirement saving opportunities.

- **Do: Find your own, subtle ways of saving money.** One of the most popular ways of saving money on your own is through "saving-challenges," which essentially requires your contribution of small amounts of money each day into your "savings fund." This might mean you add $2 every day to your fund until you retire. When you begin this at an early age, say 40, and continue it until your retire, say 65, you'll have saved $18,250. The great part? It's such a small daily contribution that it's barely noticeable.

The Don'ts of Retirement

- **Don't: Overindulge.** With retirement often comes the thought of beautiful vacation retreats, luxurious travel, and high-end purchases. While these indulgences are fine if you're in a financially comfortable position, you need to think: Will my desire for "living large" *now* result in the need for "small living" *later*? **Retiring with enough money is important, yes, but maintaining your money *throughout* retirement is equally important.**

- **Don't: Try your luck.** Purchasing a lottery ticket or planning a weekend trip to the casino is fine—with moderation. Keep in mind, though, that you've put in a tremendous effort to saving enough money so that you can retire comfortably. You don't ever want to jeopardize your hard work or your means of financial support.

- **Don't: Take money out of your 401(k) before retirement.** Even when emergencies happen, you need to avoid this at all costs. Although it *technically* is a possibility to withdraw money from your 401(k) before retirement, there are a complex set of rules, restrictions, and penalties that follow.

Conclusion

No matter what stage you're at in the retirement process, my biggest recommendation is to contact and speak with a financial expert you trust—preferable someone who specializes in retirement. You'll learn a great deal of reliable information from him or her, and will always have a dependable resource to consult if confusions or issues arise.

However, this book is designed to help you in the meantime. In Chapter 1, you hopefully discovered a better understanding for the retirement market—what financial challenges the average retiree confronts and how those challenges might be similar to the ones *you* may confront in your near—or perhaps far—future. In Chapter 2, we introduced a great calculation technique to figure out how much money you'll need to retire comfortably—saving 8x your annual income before retirement. In Chapter 3, we discussed the 401(k)—a pre-retirement saving program that all too often goes overlooked, yet is a crucial element to the retirement process. Chapter 4, then, encouraged you to take a different approach, to self-reflect on what you want your life to consist of during retirement—family and friends, travel and adventure, or something in between? You've hopefully discovered the usefulness of this step: by determining what retirement activities you wish to pursue after you stop working, you gain a better understanding for how much money you truly need to save to support yourself. Chapter 5, on the other hand, proposes a more complex idea—paying off a mortgage or debt *before* retirement. If you were wary of the benefits of doing this at first, hopefully this chapter has shown you how this step can help you retire with enough money. Lastly, Chapter 6 introduced additional ways to guarantee your financial retirement success—*do* take advantage of other investing opportunities, ask about pension options, and establish your own savings fund, but *don't* overindulge, test your luck, or withdraw savings from your 401(k).

Having read this, your next step is to put all of this information into action. Spend some time doing the retirement calculations we advised throughout this book. Determine how much money you'll need in order to retire in a financially comfortable position *before* you retire. Think about *who* you want to be after you retire and make sure your savings can support this. Your careful calculations and thoughtful self-reflections will play a major role in ensuring you can retire with enough money, whatever amount you've carefully determined that to be.

Bonus Book 2

We Paid Off Our $375,000 Mortgage in Less Than 5 Years!

12 Proven and Effective Tips We Learned That Will Help You Become Mortgage-Free Fast Without Sacrificing Your Lifestyle

Table of Contents

Keep a journal

Chapter 5: Learn to Love Lists

Types of lists

I made a list, now what?

Chapter 6: Increasing Your Income

Online and offline income resources

Chapter 7: What to Pay off First

Paying off smaller debts

Chapter 8: Refinancing

Refinancing basics

The nitty-gritty of refinancing

Chapter 9: Tackling the Principal

What is principal?

Paying back the principal

Some helpful reassurance

Chapter 10: Making Room for Adjustment

What to expect

Adjusting advice

Chapter 11: Vacations & More

The $10 challenge

The 30-Day Saving Challenge

Chapter 12:Celebrate

Chapter 13: Life After Debt

Conclusion

Introduction

Back in February 2011, my husband and I set an extremely aggressive goal for our family. We wanted to pay off our $375,000 mortgage and become 100% debt-free within 5 years. We knew it was the type of goal that people rolled their eyes at when they heard it. We knew it was the type of goal every working-class family fears and dreads. We knew it was the type of goal that puts an indescribable amount of pressure and stress upon thousands and thousands of families across the nation who attempt it. Our family was no exception. The whole experience completely changed our lives, but not in the way you'd probably think.

For thousands of families, the thought of paying off debt and mortgage is synonymous with making drastic financial and lifestyle changes. In this sense, our family was different. As we worked toward aggressively paying off our mortgage, we found ways that let us continue to do the things we enjoyed doing before we took on the oftentimes overwhelming burden of becoming mortgage free. Instead of cutting out all family vacations and activities, as many families are forced to do in similar situations, we found ways to fly our family of 4 on a business-class vacation to Thailand. We spent 3 weeks there and stayed only in 4 or 5 star hotels. We vacationed in other places, too, like Cancun and Disney, all while spending less than 25% of our income. But let me reiterate: while doing *all* of this—keeping our family connected and treating ourselves to the lifestyle we were used to and deserved—we still managed to pay off our $375,000. The amazing part? We did all of this—the memorable family vacations and simultaneous paying off of our $375,000 debt—in less than 5 years. Yes, we became mortgage free (in 4 years and 1 month to be exact!) without sacrificing life as we knew it.

I'll be the first to admit it, it sounds so incredibly impossible. Thousands of families across America *alone* struggle every day to maintain some sort of balance while paying off their debt or mortgage, yet my family is living proof that paying off debt can be done without even the slightest sacrifice to your happiness or lifestyle. I've experienced the feeling of anxiety and immeasurable financial pressure at just the thought of paying off our mortgage. I've been there, but my family and I have also managed to escape without so much as a scratch. I genuinely want this for *your* family, too, which is why I've documented my own 12 steps to becoming mortgage and debt free without sacrificing happiness, well-being, or lifestyle. I've wrote this book is for anyone who wants to finally set themselves free from the oftentimes crippling burden of debt once and for all—and fast.

Chapter 1: The Mortgage-Free Mindset

Adopting a strong and resilient mindset is perhaps the most important tip I can give to an individual or family looking to begin the process of becoming mortgage-free. Really, I think it might be. It seems simple, though, doesn't it? Anyone can wake up one morning and decide they want to pay off their debt, but it takes a certain mindset to truly act upon the simple, optimistic thought. Sure, the idea of becoming mortgage-free is an alluring prospect to anyone who seems to be drowning in debt, but it needs to be more than *just an idea*. Eliminating your mortgage or debt needs to be a commitment. It starts with modifying your mindset and perspective into one driven by commitment, dedication, and patience. It also requires your firm belief that you *can* pay off your mortgage and that the outcome *will* be worth your while. Without these components, you're almost guaranteed to give up or fail.

The mindset that started it all

My family found success because we fervently worked to adopt an accepting and resilient mindset, but before we practiced and applied these mindsets to our daily thoughts and actions, my family—my husband and I especially—had to do something else. Before we so much as tossed a single penny into our "pay off the mortgage" fund, we needed to be in agreement over our intentions. We needed to verify our equal commitment to completing the task of paying off our mortgage. In other words, we both needed to embrace **a mindset of unwavering commitment**.

Before you, too, begin to pay off your debt, let me remind you: you and your partner need—*need*—to be on the same page. Well actually, you truly need to be on the same *word* of the same page, if you want to get figurative. If one of you likes to spend and the other likes to save, paying off your mortgage or debt won't be an easy journey. Discussing your personal spending habits with your partner, deciding how you'll modify them into ones conducive to paying off your debt, and reaffirming your commitment to accomplishing the task at hand are incredibly crucial elements that I can't possibly stress enough. Paying off your debt is a team commitment that _must_ be formed *on the very start of day one.*

The mindsets you want

I've read a lot about the mindsets you need for success, for happiness, and for healthy living. It would seem a productive and sturdy mindset is the key—or least one of them—for accomplishing goals and bettering ourselves. I think the power of a productive mindset plays an equally crucial role in becoming mortgage-free as well. My family's adoption of 2 particular mindsets as we began the process of working toward our goal is what I think gave us a firm and stable foundation for successfully becoming mortgage-free in just over 4 years. We of course clung onto multiple different mindsets when we were first starting out, but we, fortunately, stumbled across a few particularly effective ones that I believe really helped us through.

Acceptance

Acknowledging your situation can and will lead to a wide variety of emotions—guilt, anger, regret, embarrassment, frustration, disappointment, sadness, helplessness. These are all perfectly normal emotions to feel, but you can't let them control you. In order to modify and fix your situation, you first need to acknowledge and accept it for what it is. I find this to be particularly true for debt. Accepting my family's situation was no easy feat, but with time, accepting our situation allowed us to progress forward. We accepted that we couldn't change our $375,000 mortgage, and by doing so, we were able to move on and look for things we *could* change.

Resilience

If I had to pick one, this is the mindset that I'd say truly got my family through the 4 year-long process of becoming mortgage-free. This is because we had to be resilient *every day* of the process. For us, applying a resilient mindset was all about problem-solving, but not in the typical way you'd think. Instead, problem-solving for my family was all about focusing on the solution, not harboring feelings of hopelessness and defeat that come from the problem. So, we focused all of our attention on ways to eliminate our mortgage. We paid no attention to our initial problem of being in a $375,000 debt. We were entirely *committed* to finding a solution.

Practice makes perfect

It's one thing to recognize that acceptance and resilience are crucial mindsets to embrace as you begin your process of becoming mortgage-free. It's another thing to actually apply them to your daily life as you work toward achieving your debt-free goal. It can be hard—my family knows this first hand. But I think our ability to achieve our debt-free goal speaks to our success, which is why I've included some brief advice below to help you on your way.

<u>Acceptance:</u>

Learning to accept your financial situation isn't something you'll find a step-by-step process for on the internet, at least not one that will automatically and flawlessly resolve your situation. Acceptance is something that we do mentally. It takes time, patience, and commitment, but it also takes practice. Unfortunately, acceptance isn't the easiest thing to practice. I'd recommend dedicating about 5 minutes of your time to some self-reflection each morning or evening. Remind yourself that what's done is done, but that accepting your situation is the first step to taking action. Start with something small. Find something else in your life that needs acceptance—something less pressing than financial matters. You'll need to learn to accept the smaller things before you can even fathom accepting the bigger things.

<u>Resilience:</u>

Resilience is like a mental muscle that needs to be created, exercised, and continuously stretched. Some of us are born with greater resilience than others, although this won't matter in the long run—it might simply mean you need to work a bit harder at embracing and adopting this mindset. It might seem simple and perhaps even irrelevant to some, but doing basic problem-solving skills in your free time can truly help build a resilient mindset needed to gain a strong mental foundation. Math problems, riddles, and even crossword puzzles found in the newspaper or online are simple remedies to help strengthen your problem-solving skill and therefore your resilience. Again, it's all about starting small. Discover the steps you need to take in order to find success with riddles and learn what it feels like to solve these smaller problems, then apply these steps to bigger issues like tackling your debt.

Chapter 2: Imagining a Mortgage-free Life

I'll be completely honest—becoming mortgage-free isn't an easy process. It takes your complete dedication and commitment. You can't simply establish an accepting and resilient mindset and then expect to pay off your debt in one fell swoop. No, paying off your mortgage or debt is all about taking baby steps. My family had to build both a sturdy mental and financial foundation before we could even *think* about paying off our mortgage. I hope I'm not making the task of paying of a mortgage or debt sound like an impossible feat—it absolutely isn't. After all, my family was able to pay off our mortgage without sacrificing our lifestyle. What I'm trying to say is that you simply can't jump into it. You need to slowly build up to paying off your mortgage. Like we just discussed in Chapter 1, you'll need to adopt particularly strong mindsets. But once you've done this, you'll need to spend some time truly *believing* that the task of paying off your mortgage or debt is possible. *Believing* you can do this comes from *imagining* a mortgage-free life.

So this is what my family did. We imagined what our life would be like without debt. My husband and I imagined how we could better support our children throughout all their future endeavors without the thought of an immense mortgage looming over our financial decisions. We'd grab a piece of paper and a pen and jot down notes of what we'd imagined. It sounds simple, and it was, but it was an incredibly powerful tool that kept my family's motivation alive.

Ideas and resources

Aside from jotting down quick notes on how we imagined our debt-free life, my family did a multitude of other things as well. Over time, our quickly scribbled self-memos evolved into habits, activities, and crafts that helped re-spark motivation and determination when we felt it starting to dissolve.

- **Make lists:** It's simple, but so incredible valuable. Ask yourself what you *want* to do when you're debt-free, and imagine how you think your life will be once you've achieved this goal. Keep an on-going list readily available—in your nightstand drawer, in your wallet, on your kitchen counter—and add to it whenever an idea pops into your head, even if it's a bit crazy. Over time your list will show the incredible opportunities that come from being debt-free, which will in turn make your list a primary source of inspiration and motivation.

- **Read success stories:** Success stories—such as this one—can be the inspirational outlet you need to finally get your plan in action. Let these stories inspire you. I remember my very first inspired moment came from a simple article I read online. It was a yahoo article called "Secrets of Extreme Savers and How They Did it," and it detailed how families, just like my own, were able to pay off their mortgage in less than 10 years. I read about how one couple lived off of only one spouse's income starting the year they were married, and put the other spouse's entire income toward paying off their 30 year mortgage in just 7 years. Reading this got me thinking: *What would it be like for my own family to live debt-free? What must it feel like not having to worry about losing our jobs or paying off our house? What could I do with my money if I didn't have to dish out a large portion of it to paying our mortgage each month?* Eventually, imagining a debt-free life became unacceptable; I wanted to—*needed* to—remember what being debt-free felt like again.

- **Imagine the future:** Dedicate some time to reflect upon what a debt-free future would entail. Embrace your daydreams. Maybe you'd be able to retire earlier and would then be able to spend more time with your children or grandchildren. Maybe a debt-free life would give you the opportunity to invest in something you feel passionate about? Perhaps you could finally buy that local bakery you've driven by looking longingly at for years. Envisioning your future gives you a *purpose*, and sometimes, a strong purpose is all you really need.

- **Create a vision board:** Visual reminders of our desires and goals are incredible outlets for inspiration and motivation. Look at the lists you've created—have you imagined more tropical family vacations after paying off your debt? Find a picture of your dream vacation spot in a magazine or print one off the internet. Add it to your vision board. Let it inspire you every time you look at it. Keep in mind that your vision board doesn't have to be anything fancy, especially if your family is already on a tight budget. Your vision board can be a poster or corkboard hung in a frequently visited household place—the living room or kitchen, for example. Your vision board should turn into a collage of the things you want or the life you imagine after becoming mortgage or debt-free. It's a constant reminder of your purpose and why you want to achieve your debt-free goal.

Chapter 3: Know Your Situation

When my family first sat down to discuss our goal of becoming mortgage-free, we struggled. However, we didn't struggle because our mindsets weren't strong enough, and we didn't struggle because we didn't properly imagine our debt-free futures. We struggled because we didn't *know* our financial situation. Yes, we knew we had a $375,000 mortgage hovering above our heads, but we had no idea what our weekly and monthly expenses were. Of course we looked at our bank statements, but we couldn't distinguish the necessary expenses from the unnecessary expenses. So, we needed to find a way to do this before we could actually work toward achieving our goal.

Still inspired by that yahoo article I read about families becoming debt-free in 7 years, I began to do some rough calculations of my own. My husband and I sat down together to review my work, and we eventually agreed that our goal was achievable if we could truly manage our expenses in an efficient and smart manner. At this point, our "becoming completely debt-free in 5 years extreme plan" was born.

Over the next couple of weeks, my family became *very* familiar with creating and utilizing spreadsheets. We discovered that in order to get where we wanted to be—out of a $375,000 debt—we had to know where we currently stood. We needed to know our current financial situation first in order to create a realistic plan and achieve our mortgage-free goal.

Who does it benefit?

Here's the thing: we too often think that high income families are able to pay off their mortgage more quickly and painlessly than families with low incomes. Although this might be true for some, it certainly doesn't hold true for thousands of families across the country. Just think about it: if a family has a high income, they might be less concerned with debt, budgeting, or sacrificing the lifestyle they've grown accustomed to. With a high income, a family might not pay close attention to their monthly expenses or where their money goes. But these habits aren't productive ones when trying to pay off their mortgage, which is why even families with high incomes need to identify and understand their financial situation—what the household income is, what the household expenses are, and what portion of the monthly income remains after bills are paid. So regardless of whether you live in a single-person household with a low income or a household of 10 with a high income, taking the time to know and understand your financial situation is crucial. Anyone and everyone—no matter their income level—will benefit from knowing where they stand financially each month. I say this because my family wasn't able to pay off our mortgage because we had a high income; we were able to pay off our mortgage in less than 5 years because we followed a series of steps and dedicated our time to truly figuring out where we stood financially each month.

Learn to love spreadsheets

Using excel spreadsheets are a free and valuable resource to take advantage of if your family finds themselves in a similar situation to ours. I'd even recommend using an excel spreadsheet even if you're completely aware of your expenses. It's a great tool that lets you track your financial situation, but it's also a great tool that reaffirms your need to remain dedicated and motivated during the process.

As you begin creating spreadsheets, you'll need to familiarize yourself with two crucial components:

- Your household's monthly income
- Your household's monthly expenses (on necessary items such as bills and groceries)

Then you'll want to know the exact breakdown of your monthly expenses. Ask yourself:

- How much of our monthly income goes to bills?
- How much of our monthly income goes to groceries?
- How much of our monthly income is left over after these necessary expenses are paid?

Once you figured this out, it's time to enter it into an excel spreadsheet. But remember, you don't need to be an expert at excel. All you need to do is press on the cells and enter the information you have. Here's a really simple example of what your income/expense spreadsheet might look like:

	Jan. income	Jan. expenses	End of Month	Feb. income	Feb. expenses	End of Month
Jane	$4,000	Bills: $2,000	$4,000-$2,800=	$5,000	Bills: $2,500	$5,000-$3,100=
		Groceries: $800			Groceries: $600	
		total: $2,800	$1,200		total: $3,100	$1,900
John	$4,000	Bills: $2,500	$4,000-$3,300=	$2,000	Bills: $2,500	$2,000-$3,100=
		Loans: $800			Loans: $800	
		total: $3,300	$700		total: $3,100	($1,100)

Simply knowing what each family member's monthly income is, what they spend monthly on expenses, and what their end of the month leftover income or loss is will be enough to get you more familiar with your financial situation. If you can think of more factors to add in or want to make your expense spreadsheet more complex, go for it. My family found that even this simple way worked wonders, so stick to whatever you're comfortable with doing. Once you see what's actually happening with your money, you'll be able to make a realistic and reasonable plan.

Chapter 4: Goals, Timelines, and Action Plans

I remember when we first set the goal to pay off our mortgage in 5 years. The number was more my idea than my husbands—this was made obvious when my husband's quizzical look evolved into one of complete shock once I explained to him our intended deadline. After about 5 minutes of staring at me as if I had sprouted 5 heads, my husband agreed to give it a try, though I still think he thought me completely insane at the time.

We started broad. We determined how many *years*—not months—we wanted to give ourselves to achieve our goal. I'd read inspirational stories about families doing it in

7 years, but I was inspired and motivated enough to do it in 5. Nonetheless, once my husband and I settled on a broad timeline, it was then time for us to get into the nitty-gritty details. At this point we'd adopted particular mindsets, spent time envisioning debt-free futures that would serve as motivation, and gained a solid understanding for our financial situation. Now was the time to start *planning*. Yes, we'd settled for a 5-year plan, but we now had to identify specific goals and milestones we would need to achieve within those 5 years. We wanted to pay off our mortgage and other debts fast, so our timeline and action plan had to be aggressive. However, we also knew the importance of finding a balance between

aggressive goal-setting and realistic goal-setting. Without both of these, I don't think our outcome would've been the success that it is.

Getting started

There were a few specific steps we took when establishing our goals, timeline, and actions:

- **Time:** Decide how long you want to give yourself to accomplish your goal. Be aggressive, but be realistic. If you have a mortgage or debt somewhat equivalent to what ours was, then you should be in the 5-10 year range. It sounds awful, I know. But you need to be honest, realistic, and patient. For smaller debts, you might want to give yourself a little less time. The opposite goes for larger debts. The rule of thumb for deciding on a time limit or deadline is this: be realistic.

- **Blueprint:** Once you've established your long-term goal, break it down into smaller steps and milestones. Set specific goals for specific years, or perhaps even specific months. My family called this process of timeline-planning "blueprinting" because it reminded us of what our overall goal was and what we had to do to get there. We set goals for how much money we wanted to put toward our mortgage-free goal each month *and* each year. We did all math beforehand so we knew exactly how much we needed to put away each month in order to meet our March 2016 goal.

- **Adjust:** When you set goals, create timelines, and develop action plans, you need to make sure they remain the same. Within the first few months it's crucial that you evaluate and adjust. If you've decided to save $10,000 each month but find that it's nearly impossible, readjust to saving only $5,000 each month. Give it a few months to see if this new goal works out—if it doesn't, adjust again until it does. If it does, stick to it. A lot of families will be tempted after the first year or two to change their goal to paying off only half of the mortgage— don't let this enticing thought creep up.

- **Plan ahead:** When we create goals and timelines, we oftentimes forget to plan ahead or consider situations that might unfortunately appear. This is why it's important that your action plan includes having an emergency fund. Hospital bills not covered by insurance are unfortunate, but they do happen, so take this into consideration as you plan ahead.

Keep a goal checklist

When my husband and I sat down to do some serious, in-depth thinking about our goals, we decided to create and keep a checklist throughout the entire process. We wanted an organized way of keeping our plan on track, but we also wanted a tangible way of seeing our progress. Our personal checklist looked something like this:

Pay-off Goals: ($375,000)

- Main mortgage

- Home equity loan

- Credit cards

By March 2016, our goals are to:

- Be completely debt-free

- Eliminate day-care expenses

- Go on vacations to dream destinations (Hawaii, Thailand, Europe, Caribbean Cruise)
- Increase incomes—at least 2 promotions (combined)
- Husband's early retirement by age 45?
- Pay off uncle and buy back our land in Thailand in my name
- Create and save for emergency fund
- Boost our savings and investing: IRA, 401K, and Mutual Fund
- ***Do all of this without changing the way we live.

You'll notice that we didn't have *just one* goal. We also has many other smaller goals that we wanted to achieve, such as eliminating the expenses of my children's day-care or buying back the land in Thailand we once owned.

Nonetheless, when we completed each goal, my husband and I would mark it in red ink as "Done." I can't explain how rewarding this simple gesture felt.

Keep a journal

From what I've seen, a lot of families struggle to get past the first year or two of their plan. The main reason why they stop? They don't notice an impressive change in their situation. Sure, they put thousands of dollars within the first year toward mortgage payments, but when their mortgage is $500,000, it doesn't really *seem* like a lot. So they stop. I get it, I really do. I understand how frustrating it is to save thousands of dollars, put it towards paying off an obscure and intangible number, and not seeing much of a change at all. I'll be the first to admit that seeing that can be a truly disheartening, pit-in-stomach feeling. I say this from experience. After the first couple months of using our savings to pay off the mortgage, we barely noticed the slightest of a difference. After all, what is $16,000 compared to $375,000? It's miniscule. It's like an ant standing next to a person. When I thought about it this way, I, too, was ready to throw my hands up in the air out of frustration and stop.

But then I did some thinking. I thought about the mindsets my family and I agreed upon early in the process. I recalled them, practiced them, and worked them back into my every day routine. I remembered my family's agreement to stay committed throughout this entire process. So, with my reaffirmed vow of commitment and my refreshed resilient mindset, I sat down and did some thoughtful and much-needed thinking.

Eventually, I decided to keep a journal. At the end of each month I would update it, making sure to record:

- Our total income for the month
- The total expenses we paid during the month
- What money we had left over after all expenses were paid

- How much money my husband and I earned from side-jobs
- How much money we put into our savings account
- How much money we took out for emergencies
- How much money we used for family activities or daytrips
- How much money we put toward paying off our mortgage
- Any additional expenses we acquired or were able to pay off that month

It was essentially a hand-written version of the excel spreadsheets we were now highly accustomed to. The only difference was that I used the journal to keep track of our progress.

I used it to remind me that we *were* actually making progress. If you're interested in seeing more, I've included some excerpts of my own personal journal in Chapter 14.

I tell you this because a journal can be a wonderful resource if you find you're drowning in frustration or feel like your efforts aren't paying off. I tell you this because something as simple as a journal can remind you of why you're doing what you're doing. If you're not convinced, here's an example of what I mean:

So, let's assume that you and your partner have managed to earn an extra monthly income in addition to putting aside specific amounts of money each month after you've paid the bills. Let's say that this amounts to $8,000 a month. (Yes, I know this can be a lot—but this is the amount it would take to pay off a $375,000 mortgage in 4 years). There's clearly a lot of wiggle room, though—setting the goal to 10 years instead of 4 would mean you need only put $4,000 toward a $375,000 mortgage payment a month, for example). Nonetheless, watch what happens in your journal if you record your updated mortgage debt each month.

Hint: You won't see a noticeable difference within the first couple of months, but after the first year, your journal *will* show something amazing.

<u>Year 1:</u>

February 2011: Owe $375,000

March 2011: $367,000

April 2011: $359,000

May 2011: $351,000

June 2011: $343,000

July 2011: $335,000

August 2011: $327,000

September 2011: $319,000

October 2011: $311,000

November 2011: $303,000

December 2011: $295,000

Within that first year alone, you'll have paid off almost $100,000 of your mortgage. But watch what happens in the following years:

Year 2:

February 2012: Owe $199,000

Year 3:

February 2013: Owe $103,000

Year 4:

February 2014: Owe $7,000

March 2014: Owe $0.00

My point is: keeping track of your month-by-month finances in a journal can be an incredibly rewarding and motivational thing.

Chapter 5: Learn to Love Lists

People use lists every day. We make lists when we go to the grocery store, when our chaotic schedules seem to grow out of control, when we need to accomplish a particular set of actions in a specific order, or when we pack for a vacation. My family used lists for all of these occasions, but we also used them during our process of becoming mortgage-free. We used them to quickly jot down ideas of how we imagined a debt-free future, and we again turned to them when my family needed to decide how to cut back on unnecessary expenses.

Types of lists

Because our goal of becoming mortgage free in 5 years was so ambitious, we decided that we wanted to put more money toward our set savings goal each month. To do this, we needed to do some cutting back—but not in the way you'd think. Some families think cutting back on expenses means sacrificing food quality or quantity—we didn't do this. Instead, we created lists of the things we absolutely couldn't live without, the things we loved so much that we simply couldn't give up, and the things we could sacrifice without also sacrificing our own happiness, well-being, and lifestyle.

You'll notice that the "need" list doesn't always need to be essentials. We decided we could still buy new running shoes when we needed them, but we also decided that we didn't need to spend $200+ on a single pair of shoes, either. We established that we could still continue our Friday night family night-out if we reduce the amount of takeout we ordered each week (which, by the way, was a cost that added up to $100 a week that we really didn't need or even appreciate anymore).

I made a list, now what?

So you've made some lists of the things you *need* and the things you *don't need.* Now what? Well, now's the time to do some analyzing. I'd recommend starting with your "don't need" list.

Look at your "don't need" list

Take a look at what you wrote down—what you don't need—and decide how you're going to cut those things out of your life. Sometimes it's a simple as not stopping at Dunkin Donuts on your way to work. Other times, however, you'll need to set a budget for yourself before you go shopping to deter you from spending a ridiculously steep amount of money on designer curtains that you really don't even need.

Look at your "need" list

Sometimes we can indulge in the things we need for a lesser cost. Let's use grocery shopping as an example. Your household obviously needs food, so groceries and food can remain on the "need" list without any guilt. But many families oftentimes buy the brand-name projects over the generic brands. Why though? Both boxes of cereal are made with the same ingredients and have nearly identical nutritional contents, yet the brand-name cereal is oftentimes twice the amount of money as the generic brand. Why not buy the generic brand? You'll buy what you *need,* and you'll save a noticeable amount of money in the process. This goes for everything else on your "need" list—get creative. Come up with creative ways to satisfy the things on your need list while spending less or not spending money at all. If you're an avid coffee drinker and don't want to give up your simple morning pleasures, then don't. You can save money while still indulging in coffee—brew your morning coffee at home ($.10 a cup) instead of buying a small cup of coffee at chain restaurants ($2.00 a cup). Still think this is a sacrifice? There are plenty of websites where you can actually buy $25 worth of gift cards at 70% off. If you enjoy taking the kids to museums, you can check out your local library—most offer free passes to excellent museums and entertainment attractions for all ages.

Chapter 6: Increasing Your Income

Within the first couple of months of establishing our goals and outcomes, my family and I realized that we might need to add an additional step if we truly wanted to pay off our $375,000 mortgage in 5 years. My husband and I were adamant about not sacrificing our family's happiness and the lifestyle our children were accustomed to, so we knew we needed to devise a plan that would let us continue to meet our monthly and yearly goals without affecting our family's well-being or making any drastic life changes.

So, we did our research. Within the first couple of minutes of generically typing in "easy ways to make an income" and "fast ways to earn money" into our internet browser, we quickly realized that there were indeed actual, legit ways to earn a little money on the side—just what our family needed to comfortably meet goals and maintain our usual lifestyle. We not only *found* ways to increase our income both online and offline; we also *utilized* these very tools.

Online and offline income resources

If you've got a particular hobby or a certain set of skills that you think you can use to your advantage—that is, if you think you can earn an income from them—then you'll find a plethora of online resources that can and will help you earn an income from the comfort of your own home. Some of the websites my own family found success with included:

- **Fiverr:** If you have unique talents or potential income-producing skills, this website is your new best friend. You can offer your services in an extensive amount of areas—graphic design, digital marketing, writing, video, animation, music, audio, programming, advertising, business, lifestyle, and gifts (there's also categories labeled "Fun & Bizarre" and "other" in case your talents don't fit under any of the categories listed above). Fiverr is filled with a friendly, large, and welcoming community of buyers and sellers, the webpage is incredibly navigable, and it takes a few short minutes to make an account and get started. So put your skills out there!

- **UpWork:** UpWork is a great resource for the beginning or expert freelancer. A simple search will bring you to pages upon pages of freelance work opportunities, which can be anything from editing an academic paper to writing articles for a major magazine company. Once you find jobs of interest, you submit a bid, a project proposal, and wait to hear back. I've personally found tremendous success using this *free* website—I'm able to work the hours I want and pick the projects I complete. And although this resource revolves around writing gigs, you'll also find that potential clients are searching for other areas of expertise and knowledge as well—there are paid opportunities just waiting for those educated in or even familiar with marketing, communication, technology, and even graphic design, so don't let your disinterest in writing deter you from checking out this extraordinarily interactive and user-friendly site.

If you already have a job or find that your schedule is just too busy to pick up additional or online work, don't worry. You can increase your current income without having to turn to online resources. Learning new skills, completing certificate-earning courses, or continuing your education (especially if your company is willing to support your educational endeavors) are all great ways to increase your salary. Learning skills that relate to your current profession is ideal. You'll gain vital experience, increase your job performance, and will allow yourself more opportunities to receive promotions and salary bumps. I say all this from personal experience—most of my extra income came from learning new skills and earning professional certifications, both of which gave me 2 off-cycle salary increases, 1 promotion, multiple bonuses, and an annual salary increase. And yes, I learned and fostered these skills from resources as simple as YouTube videos.

- **YouTube:** If you've set a tight budget but are interesting in learning new skills, look no further. I can't say enough good things about YouTube, but for starters, it's *free*. All it takes is an idea, a keyword of what you'd like to watch, and a simple click of a button. I'd usually spend just an hour a day watching videos, but within that hour I'd learn an incredible amount—I learned how to create a website using WordPress which allowed me to advertise my services and products, and I discovered how to make money using Amazon's affiliate program which I could then connect to my WordPress website I previously created. The possibilities are virtually endless, and much of what I learned during that 5 year span are still skills and resources I use today, debt-free.

What I appreciated most about advertising my skills on Fiverr and UpWork and learning new skills on YouTube was that I was not only able to support my family's endeavors of becoming mortgage-free, but that I no longer had to work for anyone else. I was my own boss. The best part was that I didn't need to pile loads and loads of money into a fancy business degree or take out a second mortgage in order to support myself and my family during the process. I found success, independence, and a mortgage-free life by utilizing these very *free* resources, online and offline.

Chapter 7: What to Pay off First

By this point, you've hopefully realized that it took some extensive thinking and planning before my family could actually start paying off our mortgage. We didn't simply wake up one morning and decide that we wanted to set this aggressive and ambitious goal. We knew from the very start that it would be—that it would *need* to be—a slow progress. Envisioning a debt-free future, establishing aggressive yet realistic goals, and actively working toward securing an additional income were important elements to my family. We truly believed that our success would come from a solid foundation and unwavering patience. I still believe this.

After we created a successful foundation, we sat down to discuss the next step. *Is it finally time to make those large mortgage payments?* We tossed around this idea for quite some time, but finally decided we weren't quite at that stage yet. A few more things needed to be done first. For starters, we needed to pay off our other, smaller debts.

Considering the current economy, most families, including mine, have other debts beside mortgages. Student loans and credit card debts are some of the most popular yet equally crippling culprits, but debts come in many other varieties as well, as I'm sure many of you are well aware of. So, how did my husband and I go about paying off our other debts before tackling our mortgage?

Paying off smaller debts

First and foremost, don't let the thought of multiple debts bog you down. This is where that accepting and resilient mindset we discussed in Chapter 1 comes into play. Refresh and re-strengthen your mindsets, then return to the situation at hand. My family found tremendous success by doing the following:

Credit card debt

You're probably not going to like this piece of advice, but it's crucial—take an inventory of all your credit cards. Record how much you owe on each card including the interest rate, and remember, don't freak out. You can't tackle the issue unless you know just how much of an issue it is. Fortunately, credit card debt is a somewhat negotiable thing. No, you won't be able to convince your contract issuer that they should forget about the $10,000 you owe, but you can negotiate a lower interest rate on each of your cards (with the right amount of smooth-talking and patience, of course). It's kind of a ridiculous thing, but reducing your interest rate by a few points can have a drastic effect on how much you actually need to pay off. In the meantime, avoid using your cards—credit and debit, for that matter—at all cost. It'll be counterproductive to pay off your credit card debt(s) while you're still actively charging them.

Student loans

Student loans can be harsh, unforgiving, and mercifulness thing, but with the right resources and qualifications, escape might actually be a possibility. I'd highly recommend reviewing the following sites to see if your situation applies:

- **Public Service Loan Forgiveness Program:** Finally, a potential escape. Most people have never heard of this, which is quite unfortunate because if you qualify—if you're employed by the government or a non-profit organization, among a few other elements—you might be able to secure variations of loan forgiveness. It's definitely worth a try, so here's the link:

- https://studentaid.ed.gov/sa/repay-loans/forgiveness-cancellation/public-service

- **SponsorChange.org:** Essentially, the idea is this: you volunteer for specific projects and causes and SponsorChange will help you chip away at your student loan. Finding volunteer projects in your area (you can search by entering your zip code) can be difficult depending on where you live, but it's definitely worth your time and effort if it'll help you pay off that pesky student loan. Here's the link:

- o http://www.sponsorchange.org/

Chapter 8: Refinancing

With the looming prospect of paying off smaller debts in our past, my family was finally—*finally*—able to start the long-awaited process of paying off our mortgage. However, this didn't mean we just started to make larger monthly payments. Instead, we looked into our refinancing options.

For many families, especially for young couples who are just starting out, the thought of refinancing can be somewhat frightening. When I bought my first house, I had no idea what refinancing was, and I'm sure many families are in a similar boat. But let me reassure you, refinancing isn't as awful or intimidating as many people make it sound. In fact, my family and I found quite a bit of success in learning about the process and actually refinancing our home. I'm certainly no expert, but I've been through the process multiple times and have a few helpful suggestions if you find yourself leaning toward this option as well.

Refinancing basics

Sometimes we make it out to be a bigger issue than it really is, but essentially, refinancing works like this:

- Borrowers add up the total amount of their home loans. If the current value of your home is more than the value of your total loans, you can look into refinancing your loans into **one.**

- When you refinance, you get a new mortgage that essentially replaces the original mortgage. When you do this, you're paying the interest rate for *one* loan, not two. If done correctly, you have the potential to save a considerable amount of money.

- It's a great option for borrowers with perfect or excellent credit—you can convert a variable loan rate to a fixed and lower interest rate, which is always ideal.

The nitty-gritty of refinancing

Our experience with multiple refinancing was great. The amount of money we saved on interest rates was money we put toward our vacations savings and emergency fund. However, refinancing isn't always the right option for everyone, so one of my top recommendations is to do your research. Dedicate time to reading articles and essays about refinancing your home. Set up a time to meet with your bank or a banking representative you trust. In the meantime, I'd recommend spending some time skimming and reading the helpful link I've provided below. Refinancing can get a bit complicated if you're not entirely sure about the refinancing process, but reading this article will spur questions or concerns that you can bring up during your next meeting. Here's the link:

❖ http://www.mortgagecalculator.org/hel

pful-advice/what-is-a-refinancing.php

Chapter 9: Tackling the Principal

As you're probably beginning to gather, the first couple of months of our becoming-mortgage-free process was filled with a lot of different actions. We had to admit our faulty mindsets then replace them with ones more conducive to ensuring our success. We had to understand and track our current financial situation before we even began to envision a new one. We had to determine specific goals for ourselves that were both aggressive yet reasonable—a more challenging process than some may think. We created excel spreadsheets, lists of the lifestyle habits we simply couldn't sacrifice, and journaled about our feats and defeats. We found resources that secured additional monthly incomes so that we could maintain our current lifestyle while also setting aside some additional money for our savings. We paid off credit card debts and refinanced multiple times. We did a tremendous amount within those first couple months, and an even greater amount in that first year. Yet there was still more to do. At this point, we now needed to begin the actual pay-off process. This process started with tackling the nitty-gritty aspect of a mortgage—the principal.

What is principal?

When I bought my first home, I wasn't too familiar with the structure of a mortgage. Sure, I knew the basics: a mortgage is a long-term loan intended to help home-buyers purchase a house. What I learned soon after, however, was that there are 4 different elements that, unfortunately, tag along with a mortgage—interest, tax, insurance, and principal. I already had a fairly comprehensive understanding of what the first three elements were, but I was a bit unsure about the latter. For young or new home-owners that find themselves in the same boat I was once in, a principle is essentially:

- The amount of money that you borrowed from your lender and have to pay back.

Paying back the principal

Because my husband and I were determined to have our family maintain the same lifestyle we were accustomed to before we began this process, we worked hard to bring in side-incomes throughout the entire process. I was actively discovering, learning, and practicing new skills from free resources so that I could advertise my services and profit from them. Because of this, my family had an extra inflow of money each month that we decided to set aside in order to make extra payments to the principal.

Our initial goal was to add $5,000 to the principal every 2 months, which would mean we would be done paying off our loan before the end of 2012.

I think our success in paying off our mortgage in less than 5 years came from a combination of things, but I think turning our full attention during the first year to paying off the principal played a very active role in our success. This is why I strongly recommend that you start with paying off the principal. Here's what I'd suggest:

- Make paying off the principal (and it's interest, too) your main priority. When you tackle this challenge aggressively, much like we did, you save an incredible amount of money on interest. Interest can be a killer, especially when you don't tackle it head on, so think about it this way: the lower your principal, the less money you dish out to interest each month. Make the principal (and the insane interest that comes with it) your enemy. Make aggressive payments and try with all your might to force it out of your financial equation.

- At the end of each month, combine the money you saved and earned, and put it toward paying off the principal. This can be the money you received from:
  - o Salary increases
  - o Annual bonuses
  - o Incomes from part-time, freelance, or side-jobs

o   Tax refunds

Our family thrived when we followed these above steps. From just salary increases, annual bonuses, and paying off loans, we were saving an extra $1,100 a month, a large chunk of money that we put toward paying off our principal faster (which also meant we were increasing our interest). I've included a few excerpts of my personal journal to help show just how effective these simple financial changes were in helping us pay off our principal and mortgage faster.

Tuesday, March 1, 2011:

My husband received a 4% salary increase and I received a 4.73% salary increase. With our new salaries combined, we now earn an extra $400 a month!

Friday, March 4, 2011:

Today we paid off our land loan using the $5,000 we got back from Dependent Care and my husband's bonus money. Paying off our land loan means we decreased our monthly expenses by $770. That's huge! With our extra $400 a month from salary increases and our $770 savings a month from paying off our land loan, we're now saving an extra $1,100 per month <u>without changing a thing!!</u>

I hope this shows just how easy it can be to find money to put toward the principal payments. I also have a few other suggestions as you focus on paying off your principal:

- If you've established an emergency fund, don't take money from this source. You should always have some emergency savings readily available in case, god forbid, something unexpected unfortunately happens.

- If your family has set up a specific monthly budget that goes toward family activities or vacation, don't pull money from this savings source, either. This separate savings account was especially important to my family, so we essentially ignored its existence when it came time to make mortgage payments. (If you're interested in learning more about our vacation savings fund, be sure to check out Chapter 11).

Some helpful reassurance

I'll be completely honest. When you first start paying off your principal, it's going to look like you send all of your money to the bank. Actually, it's kind of true. It's going to be frustrating, and you're going to discover that your motivation will run thin. But I can also tell you that doing this will pay off in the end. Keep in mind that this is temporary—once you pay off your mortgage, everything you earn from that point on is YOURS. Aside from paying your weekly or monthly utility and grocery bills, your income will go in your pocket. You'll be able to do as you wish with your money without the looming thought of a mortgage hanging over your head.

Chapter 10: Making Room for Adjustment

Although my family was able to maintain the lifestyle we were already used to throughout the entire process of becoming mortgage free, it was still a big change for us. Sure, we continued to indulge in the family activities and vacations we felt strongly about keeping, but staying on top of your financial spreadsheets, juggling our careers with side jobs, and tackling the principal payments up front required extra attention that we weren't yet used to. With that being said, the first few months of this entire process were hard—not impossibly hard—but pretty hard. But it wasn't hard because paying off our mortgage was an impossible task, and it wasn't because we lacked the resources we needed to successfully manage the payments. It was hard because it was something we just weren't used to. It was a foreign process. Our mortgage had technically left us in $375,000 debt with our lender, but we didn't really notice the amount of debt we were truly in until we started sending those large principal payments to the bank. We weren't used to living off of my husband's income alone, and we certainly weren't used to sending my entire monthly income and our combined side incomes all to the bank, never to be seen again. This alone definitely took some getting used to, especially when the payments didn't really seem to make a dent on our mortgage at first.

Fortunately, we foresaw that this might happen. When we first began the process, we knew that adjusting to this new budget and saving-orientated lifestyle would be, well, a process. My family understood from the start that we simply couldn't throw ourselves into this new routine without setting aside some time for adjustment. My husband and I found success in paying off our mortgage, in part, because we planned ahead. We knew that the first couple of months would be hard, so we factored that into our plan. But here's some reassurance: it got easier after the first couple of months. I'll be completely honest—I don't think a family can undergo this process without experiencing some difficulties in the first few months, though this is perfectly normal. But once you get into the routine of paying off your principal in large chunks and you begin to see the amount of your mortgage go down, you'll find a new kind of motivation—one that reaffirms your commitment and sparks your desire to progress. Once you get past this adjustment period, I promise the entire process will become much easier.

What to expect

I'm certainly not an expert on these things—I can only speak from my own family's experience and from what others in similar situations have told me. However, I think my family's experience can be really telling. We didn't necessarily have the same experience with paying off our mortgage as other families—we did it so aggressively without sacrificing any of the things we truly cared about, though I'm sure others out there have found similar success—but I think my family's experience can accurately give your family a heads-up about what to expect during the process of paying off a mortgage or debt. Here's what we'd say:

- **Expect to feel frustrated at times.** My family experienced unusual success throughout this experience, but that doesn't mean we didn't get frustrated throughout the 4 years and 1 month we were committed to our plan. Sometimes my husband and I got frustrated, for example, because it killed us to see the monetary rewards of our hard work go directly to an intangible account at the bank.

- **Expect to feel like you're efforts aren't noticeable.** As I mentioned earlier, the first couple of principal payments will barely show a change in your mortgage or debt. It *will* seem like you're sending loads of money into thin air. It's the unfortunate truth, but it *is* the truth. What's also true, however, is that it *will* pay off and it *will* begin to show if you stick to it. What I'm trying to say is this: your efforts may not be noticeable at first, but those same efforts become crucial and vital to your success the moment you pursue them.

- **Expect to feel like you want to give up.** Paying off a debt this large is absolutely a trying task, especially within those first couple of months when you haven't yet settled into some sort of payment routine. My best advice is this: take this process one month at a time, one week at a time, and even one day at a time—whatever you need to do to keep your sanity. Viewing your task as a 10-year monetary prison sentence won't help you in any way. Break your goal down into manageable sections. Push throw when you face those rough patches at the beginning. Know that things *will* get easier when you fall into a routine.

Adjusting advice

Even though my family factored in a 3-5 month adjustment period, we did face our share of difficulties. The truth is that paying of a debt of anything over $50,000 is no small feat. No matter how much you prepare, things *will* have the tendency to get in your way. For us, this was the adjustment period. We had spent so much time planning that we thought the entire process would go smoothly. And it did, until we were 4 months into the adjustment period and experienced the feelings of frustration sneak up on us. Luckily, we noticed this in time before our commitment and motivation suffered or was compromised.

My family had a few discussions during this adjustment period. We checked in with each other, reaffirmed our unanimous commitment, and sparked our original motivation. We eventually fell into a routine at around the 6 month mark, and all was good.

However, I'm sure many families have also reached this point and have struggled to get through it. Again, I'm certainly no expert on adjustment, but I can tell you what worked best for my family during this adjustment period.

- **Maintain strong and supportive relationships with family members.** A lot of families have the tendency to break down during trying times, especially when it involves financial matters. You can't let this happen to you. Think of your family as a team—if even one person fails to reciprocate the much-needed support during this process, the team—your family—potentially crumbles. Lean on each other for support and openly discuss your feelings and opinions during the process. Communication is an absolute must, so communication needs to happen often.

- **Be open-minded.** For my family, the adjustment period was all about going with the flow, which requires an open mind. We didn't know what to expect during this transitional period of our lives, so we needed to embrace what we were dealt. We needed to accept what we were confronted with and then simply move on.

- **Communicate.** Success—at anything, really—stems from our ability to communicate effectively with those around us. This same idea applies to your family. Sometimes coping with this adjustment period will require you to sit down with each other to discuss how you're handling your situation. One family member might be adapting to your current situation more efficiently and productively than others. If someone seems to be excelling, ask them how they've been able to do this—do they view the situation in a different way than everyone else? Do they keep a journal that lets them release their frustrations in a healthy and controlled manner? Have they found support from others outside of the family who have already gone through the situation?

- **Patience.** For my family, our adjustment period lasted about 4-6 months. This doesn't mean it's abnormal if your family adjusts quicker or slower than ours, however. In fact, my husband and I adjusted at different paces, just like my children adjusted at different speeds. And my children adjusted at different speeds when compared to my husband and I. The thing is that everyone adjusts differently. Essentially, it all comes down to patience.

Chapter 11: Vacations & More

Early on in the planning process, my family decided that we didn't want to sacrifice family vacations or fun day trips during the process of paying off our $375,000 mortgage. We valued and appreciated familial bonding time and experiences, so budgeting vacations into our plan was a must. The question was: how would we possible do this? Well, I spent some time browsing forums and searching the web for other families that had gone through a similar mortgage and debt pay-off process. Much of what I found, however, wasn't very helpful. The forums discussed the importance of "responsible financial budgeting" which didn't include vacations. Articles that I found on the web suggested some helpful websites that offered daily discounts for tropical vacations, but they oftentimes weren't to the destinations we as a family wanted to put money toward. I think many families struggle to achieve their goal of becoming debt-free, and in the process, compromise the well-being and happiness of their family, a big no-no for my husband and I.

I did some thinking. I had my heart set on taking my family to Thailand on a vacation, but I lacked the resources I needed to successfully do this. So, I did some more thinking. *How could my husband and I set aside a relatively small amount of money each month that would go toward a vacation fund?*

Many families want to set aside vacation savings, but they struggle to find ways of doing so without compromising their mortgage pay-off plan. My family found a way of doing this flawlessly, and I hope your family finds the same success.

Collect Your Free Rewards

Here's the thing: my husband and I didn't actually *save* up for vacations. All of our travel expenses—plane tickets for international business class, vacations to Disney, adventures to Cancun, bookings at 4 or 5 star hotels—were covered by using credit card points and airline miles. My husband and I were no longer charging our cards in the way we once were at this point, but we had racked up an incredible amount of "miles" over the years. I can't give an exact number, but my husband and I believe we paid 5-10% of the *actual price* for most of these tickets, hotel bookings, and vacations. Yes, that's right, it's like we were getting a 90% coupon with the credit card points and airline miles that had built up over the years.

If you're in a financial position where you can responsibly use credit cards, I'd recommend getting your hands on a travel credit card—or any credit card, really—that offers free miles for every purchase you make. You probably won't have nearly enough miles for huge family vacations within the first year or two, but it's a great investment nonetheless, especially for families who are happy to go on small, quaint, weekend trips nearby.

However, I know how tempting charging a credit card can be. This might not be the right option for everyone, and that's perfectly okay. The good news is that there are plenty of other ways to save up for much needed family vacations. I've included 2 of my personal favorites below, ones that every family—no matter their financial position or limits—will find tremendous success with.

The $10 challenge

The goal, just like it sounds, is to put $10 of your weekly paycheck toward a "vacation" or "fun" fund. The money that you use to follow this simple yet highly effective savings activity can come from the paycheck of your main job or any side-incomes you've acquired during the process. This activity is great because:

- Putting $10 a week into your vacation or "fun" saving fund is virtually an unnoticeable amount in the grand scheme of things, especially if you're paying off a debt of $50,000 or more.

- If you're an avid coffee-drinker, reducing your weekly coffee consumption by just 5 cups will give you this extra $10 a week. If you can't seem to ditch your coffee, try home-brewing— a cup of home brewed coffee will cost you about $.20 while a store-bought coffee will cost you around $2.00.

- Setting aside $10 a week adds up to $40 a month, which adds up to $480 a year.

- If you're married, have your partner do the same. You'll double your savings— $20 a week will go to your savings, which adds up to $80 a month, which adds up to $960 a year.

Here's what a year-by-year breakdown of the $10 saving plan looks like:

With 1 person saving $: week:	With 2 people saving $10 a week:
Year 1: $480 saved	Year 1: $960 saved
Year 2: $960 saved	Year 2: $1,920 saved
Year 3: $1,440 saved	Year 3: $2,880 saved
Year 4: $1,920 saved	Year 4: $3,840 saved
Year 5: $2,400 saved	Year 5: $4,800 saved

The 30-Day Saving Challenge

For those with a little more monetary and financial wiggle room, you might want to tackle this short and sweet, yet highly rewarding 30-day challenge. It's definitely a challenge, especially as you get closer to completion, but it's certainly doable with the right amount of dedication and determination.

	Deposit	Balance
Day 1	$1	$1
Day 2	$2	$3
Day 3	$3	$6
Day 4	$4	$10

Day 5	$5	$15
Day 6	$6	$21
Day 7	$7	$28
Day 8	$8	$36
Day 9	$9	$45
Day 10	$10	$55
......	......	......
Day 22	$22	$253
Day 23	$23	$276
Day 24	$24	$300
Day 25	$25	$325
Day 26	$26	$351
Day 27	$27	$378
Day 28	$28	$406
Day 29	$29	$435

Day 30	$30	$465

Why this challenge is great: By following this simple pattern, you'll have saved $465 in just 30 days. If that's not good enough, try thinking about this challenge from a different perspective:

- If you complete this challenge each month, you'll save:
    - $1,395 in 3 months
    - $2,790 in 6 months
    - $5,580 in one year
- If both you *and* your partner each complete this challenge, you'll save:
    - $930 **a month**
    - $2,790 in 3 months

- $5,580 in 6 months

- $11,160 in one year

- If both you and your partner continue this challenge for 5 years, you'll save:

  - $55,800 in 5 years....that's crazy

If both you and your partner follow this 30-day challenge, you'll be able to take your family (let's say your family of 4) on a 5-star vacation in just 3 months. Although I'd absolutely recommend using these challenges to save up for family vacations and activities so that your family can still enjoy life as you pay off your mortgage, I'd also recommend using any extra cash not spent on vacations to pay off your mortgage. These saving activities are great resources to budget out money for family vacations, but if you have some money left over, use it wisely. The sooner you eliminate your mortgage all together, the sooner you can take your family on vacation without having to complete these awesome 30-day saving challenges or setting aside $10 a week from your income.

Chapter 12:Celebrate

On May 1, 2015, our family finally became mortgage and debt-free. This was a huge win for us. We worked so very hard during that 4 year and 1 month period to accomplish our aggressive and incredibly ambitious goal of wiping out our mortgage and credit card debt entirely. Obviously a grand celebration was in order.

My family did in fact celebrate once we successfully achieved this impressive feat, but we did something different throughout the process of paying off our mortgage that I think other families don't usually do—we celebrated *before* and *during* the process of paying it off. This was crucial. We were aware that other families who have attempted this same goal viewed this process as a dreadful and burden-filled necessity. Working to achieve their goal with that mindset and perspective of their situation in mind oftentimes resulted in their failure to maintain the motivation, determination, and commitment they needed to find success. My family knew that we couldn't fall victim to this, so we celebrated. Frequently.

We celebrated our decision to make this life-changing goal a part of our daily lives for the next 5 years. We celebrated when we hit even the smallest of milestones—when my husband and I received 4% salary increases in March 2011, when my children entered school full-time and we no longer needed to spend money on day-care expenses, when we eagerly accepted promotions at work, and when I received another 12% salary increase in May 2013 (just to name a few). We celebrated quite often, regardless of whether our accomplishments were big or small. Celebrating our minor successes kept our motivation alive and our commitment strong.

I should point something out here, though. For my family, celebrating our achievements along the way didn't mean we went out for expensive dinners frequently or treated ourselves to luxurious treats. Actually, many of our frequent celebrations were quite small—my husband and I would grab a quick dinner at a local restaurant, make time to see a movie we've been too busy to watch, or get together for a cup of coffee and talk about our accomplishments. I don't want my readers to think that a celebration needs to be something extravagant. It certainly doesn't, especially when you decide to do it often. It just needs to be something inexpensive but *nice*. It needs to be something that allows your family to reflect upon your accomplishments so far, and optimistily look toward the future.

So that's my advice: celebrate before, during, and after you become mortgage-free. Why? You have so many reasons to celebrate. While other families continue to drain thousands of dollars into bank payments, your family is taking admirable actions to cut yourself loose from financial restraints and become financially free. As you celebrate even the smallest of milestones, you'll truly see and appreciate just how far along you've come. This will inspire you and keep your motivation strong, but it'll also remind you of all your hard work. After all, becoming mortgage-free is no small feat.

Chapter 13: Life After Debt

During the writing of this book, it's been almost a year since my family started our mortgage-free life. And so far, it's been one of our best. Although we have accomplished such an impressive feat—though I think I'm biased—there were a few changes we had to get used to. However, these weren't bad changes. Actually, we loved every second of these new life changes.

First and foremost, the biggest difference in our lives after we became mortgage-free was the amount of money we were saving each month. Before, large chunks of our money— most of my paycheck, actually, went to our mortgage payment and other debts like credit cards and daycare expenses. But once we finished paying these off, all the money we earned—besides the money we used to pay bills and indulge ourselves with—went right into our bank account. Money no longer vanished into intangible bank accounts, never to be seen again. We had the incredible pleasure of watching our money pile up in your savings account each month—and fast. During the 5 year-long process, we were putting an average of $10,000 per month toward paying the principal—it was a very aggressive amount of money. But when we finally reached our mortgage-free goal, the $10,000 a month that we were before putting toward the principal and mortgage instead came to our bank account. The best thing about this? The money *stayed* there until we—yes, we, not the bank—wanted to do something—anything—with it. It was such an indescribable feeling watching our hard-earned money quickly accumulate month after month. It still is.

My husband and I are still working, but it's now by choice. We do what we love and we do what we feel most passionate about. Financial insecurity, dependency, and the fear of unemployment have now been completely erased from our lives—completely obliterated. With a $375,000 mortgage constantly looming over our family of 4, my husband and I would spend innumerable sleepless nights imagining what we would do if we both lost our jobs in this current economy and fretting over how we would pay our expenses should we, god forbid, find ourselves in that dreaded financial situation. I'm sure millions of families around the world know this exact feeling and have experienced these bouts of insecurity themselves. I'm sure many families have experienced the same sleepless nights that my husband and I once experienced, and I'm sure many families have experienced the sleep-filled nights that still manage to bring with them financial nightmares. These terrors are a thing of our past now, fortunately. I don't miss them in the slightest.

Our financial mindsets have changed completely as a result of this 4-5 year process as well. When I used to envision our lives without a mortgage at the beginning of this process, I also imagined that we would have this grand celebration, throw our extra money at anything and everything we desired, and pay full price for high-end designer products without a care in the world, all because we knew we could now afford to. As it turns out, however, financial habits are hard to break. Fortunately, our current financial habits are geared toward saving money and spending it wisely. It's a habit my family definitely can't complain about. It's a good thing, really. I'm appreciative that the past 4-5 years have shaped us into economic and smart spenders. Of course without a mortgage looming over our heads we don't feel guilty indulging in the random shopping trip or buying new household objects. Yet, we continue to do these things wisely. We still actively look for deals and coupons so that we can indulge in the things we want while also being financially smart and responsible about it.

Again, old habits are hard to break, which is why my husband and I have recently developed a new goal for our family—investing our money. Since we started doing this, we've been able to take greater risks that we weren't financially allowed to do before. We've added more money into our 401K, opened a Roth

IRA, became active in peer-to-peer lending, engaged in real estate, and even bought stocks.

So what *fun* things did we do with our money? For starters, we've purchased solar panels for our house worth over $25,000—in cash, of course. Again, habits are hard to break, so we've avoided charging our credit cards like we did before. We've hired a housekeeper who comes to help out with cleaning every month. It's small, but it saves our family the time and hassle, which I think we deserve after our 4 years and 1 month of incredible hard work. We've since then also traveled back to Thailand for 3 weeks, booked business-class airplane tickets, and stayed in 4-5 star hotels.

Again, we did all of this while spending our money responsibly.

We've also recently created a "fun account" which we use for different activities—personal investing, putting money toward our businesses, donating to charities, or anything else we wish to do with it. The best part is that we don't need to check with each other about what we put our money toward, which gives me the much-needed and much-deserved sense of monetary freedom I haven't been able to fully engulf myself in throughout the past 5 years.

As for my husband, he can pretty much retire whenever he wants to. During the 5 year process of becoming mortgage-free, we trained ourselves to live on only one income,—his—but without any debt looming over our heads, we have much more monetary flexibility. However, we've discussed the potential and have recently decided, as I mentioned earlier, to install another 5 year goal. This time, we plan to spend the next 5 years building strong financial foundations by saving and investing regularly. We plan to work on our businesses and to increase our own incomes so that we can both free ourselves from the corporate world entirely and follow our passions without restraint. So essentially, our next goal is to do what we love and live the lives we love **on our own terms.**

As for me personally, entrepreneurship is a major part of my post-mortgage life. I'm now able to take more risks and invest in businesses without being crippled or restrained by a conservative budget. The self-learning I accomplished (for free) from YouTube and at the local library during the past 5 years has proven to be an incredibly rewarding experience. I apply the knowledge and skills that I learned through self-learning every single day to the businesses that I am currently growing. These invaluable skills will always be with me, and that right there is priceless to me—it's not something I was ever able to learn in a classroom.

Conclusion

Millions of families across the globe struggle with debt every day. The tricky part with debt, though, is that the degree of debt with each family varies. Some families are in debt after purchasing a $500,000 home, but have stable careers that can and will help them pay off their debt. Others on the other hand, don't. They might have relatively small debts of $100,000 or $200,000, yet they struggle more than the family with the $500,000 debt because they lack secure jobs or side incomes. Debt, no matter what form your own personal debt takes, is a fickle, tricky burden. It doesn't have to be, though. I hope my own family's experience with paying off our mortgage begins to show you this.

My family is just one of the thousands of families across America *alone* that has taken on the oftentimes intimidating challenge of paying off a home mortgage and debt. Like many other families, we had to—at first resentfully—realize that we were in debt. We had to confront our current financial situations and burdens head on and we had to refinance our home multiple times. But what separates my family from many others is the way we tackled this challenge. We adopted positive mindsets conducive to our success. We imagined what our debt-free future would look like and held onto these optimistic visions in any possible way we could—through notes quickly scribbled on lunch-break napkins, journals tucked away in our bedside drawers, or with the help of our mortgage-free vision board centrally located in the kitchen for all to see and dreamily gaze upon. We took the time to sit down and outline extensive and aggressive, yet realistic goals, timelines, and action plans. We actively searched for and landed ways to bring in side incomes each month, using the money we earned from these sources, along with bonuses when we received them, to pay off smaller credit card debts. We became refinancing experts and tackled the principal payments rather aggressively. Yet during all of this, we discreetly stashed small amounts of our weekly income into our vacation fund. My family was adamant about not changing our lifestyle in the slightest. And we never did.

My family tackled and overcame the seemingly impossible challenge of becoming debt-free after only 4 years and 1 month. We were the exception, but fortunately, we don't have to be. There are so many small and feasible ways in which any family can tackle their debt without making sacrifices to the life they've established for themselves. I've provided the exact ways in which my family did so, and I ardently hope my explanations and suggestions will or have made some sort of impact on you and your family's success.

The peace of mind my family now entertains is one every hardworking individual and family fully deserves. I wish you the best of luck in all your future endeavors.

www.ingramcontent.com/pod-product-compliance
Lightning Source LLC
Chambersburg PA
CBHW070226190526
45169CB00001B/92